PANORAMA OF WORLD ART

———

RENAISSANCE and MANNERIST ART

RENAISSANCE and MANNERIST ART

Text by ROBERT ERICH WOLF

and RONALD MILLEN

HARRY N. ABRAMS, INC. / NEW YORK / LONDON

Front end papers:

Jacopo Pontormo. Study for a lunette at the Medici Villa of Poggio
a Caiano. c. 1521. Drawing. Gabinetto Disegni, The Uffizi, Florence

Back end papers:

Polidoro da Caravaggio. Perseus with the Head of Medusa. Drawing.
The Louvre, Paris

Contents

Introduction

There is a youthful insolence about the Renaissance. Its spokesmen blithely rewrote history to make it appear that the sun rose for the first time on the first morning of their new Golden Age. The plan could not be simpler: there was a Garden of Eden called Greece and Rome; then the Fall and Expulsion which produced some eight or nine centuries of darkness; and finally a "reawakening" or, even, a "rebirth" which took place on a specific spot in Tuscany on a specific day when the talent of a boy named Giotto was discovered by a painter named Cimabue:

The Christian faith triumphed in the time of Emperor Constantine and Pope Sylvester. Idolatry was persecuted with such rigor that all the statues and pictures of great nobility, antiquity, and perfection were smashed or torn to bits. And along with the statues and pictures were destroyed the books, commentaries, drawings, and manuals which taught such an eminent and worthy art. And then, to wipe out every trace of the old customs of idolatry, it was decreed that all the churches must be white. Severe penalties were inflicted on anyone who made a statue or a picture. Thus there ended the arts of sculpture and of painting and everything men knew about them. Art died, and the churches remained white for some six hundred years. Then the Byzantine Greeks began again the art of painting, but in a most feeble manner and most crudely. As skillful as were the Ancients, so in that age were artists rough and uncouth in their art.... The art of painting began to rise again in Etruria [Tuscany]. In a village near Florence called Vespignano was born a boy of wondrous talent....He [Giotto] was the harbinger of the new art. LORENZO GHIBERTI, Il Secondo Commentario, c. 1447.

What first aroused the torpid minds from centuries of slumber was the discovery and imitation of the "perfect" art of the Ancients, the "original forms" that God had set as models for the "true" artist:

... in 1250 Heaven took compassion on the fine minds that the Tuscan soil was producing every day, and directed them to the original forms. For although the preceding generations had before them the remains of arches, colossi, statues, pillars or carved stone columns which were left after the plunder, ruin and fire which Rome had passed through, yet they could never make use of them or derive any profit from them until the period named. Those who came after were able to distinguish the good from the bad, and abandoning the old style they began to copy the ancients with all ardour and industry. GIORGIO VASARI, Le Vite de' più eccellenti pittori, scultori e architettori, 1568, translated by A. B. Hinds, 1900.

In this schematic view of history, what no one much cared to face was why, after Giotto, artists had slipped back into the bad old ways, into the "rude and rough style" which today we call International Gothic and consider an art of the most exacerbated formalistic refinement. It was against that style, after all, that the Renaissance revolted. But it was clear that a second discovery, that of Nature, combined with the discovery of Antiquity to awaken the sleepers once and for all, and that this came about in the generation of Masaccio, Brunelleschi, Ghiberti, Donatello, and Uccello:

... Masaccio entirely freed himself from Giotto's style, his heads, draperies, buildings, nudes, colouring and foreshortening being in a new manner... [with] natural attitudes, a much better expression of the emotions of the spirit and of the gestures of the body, joined to a constant endeavour to get nearer to the truth of Nature in design, while the faces are exactly like those of men as they were seen and known by the artists. Thus men sought

6

to reproduce what they saw in Nature and no more. . . . This encouraged them to make rules for perspective, and to get their foreshortening in the exact form of natural relief, proceeding to the observation of shadows and lights, shading and other difficulties, composing their scenes with greater regard for probability, attempting to make their landscapes more like reality, as well as the trees, grass, flowers, air, clouds and other natural phenomena.   GIORGIO VASARI, *Le Vite . . ., translated by A. B. Hinds.*

This, of course, was the Italian view of what happened, and it was restricted not merely to Italy but to Florence itself. Viewed from abroad, the rebirth took in a vaster territory:

In past times they had not the slightest notion of good design, nothing either reasonable or even tolerable, and thus art fell entirely into decadence. But not many years ago it was resuscitated and restored by Italy and Flanders . . .   FELIPE DE GUEVARA, Comentarios de la Pintura, *c. 1560.*

In some ways the Northern achievement was more remarkable. Much more than Masaccio and his fellows,

Maerten van Heemskerck (1498–1574). The Colossus of Rhodes, from *Icones Variae*, 1570. Engraved by Philipps Galle. British Museum, London. (Photo courtesy Witt Library, Courtauld Institute of Art, London.)

the generation of Jan van Eyck and Rogier van der Weyden was tied to a still very vital Gothic tradition. For them, there could be no guide save Nature in the rediscovery of man and his world, since Netherlandish soil held no remains of the Ancients to study and copy, none of those

beautiful marbles and bronzes which brought new light to art, opened the eyes of its adepts and taught them to distinguish the beautiful from the ugly through acquaintance with what is most perfect in all Creation, not only in human form but in the forms of animals. Armed with such a potent resource, the Italians were able to arrive very early at a correct conception of the truth of Nature, whereas we Flemings had to drudge away at it, with no other model than the common Nature which we saw about us, remaining still plunged in darkness or, at best, with only the dimmest of lights... KAREL VAN MANDER, Het Schilderboek, *1604.*

Cast on its own resources, the Northern imagination peered closely at the real things of the world, drew and painted them with a microscopic exactitude. Out of the poetry of everyday things it created its own deep poetry, often symbolic or moralistic though without the subtle intellectual overtones which the Humanists brought to Italian art. Fantastic as Netherlandish art might be, it made its impact precisely through its clear-eyed observation of reality. That is why Netherlandish art reached its greatness in two spheres: in the expression of religious feeling, and in the rendering of the world in which men live. What today we recognize as its virtues were held in small esteem by the Humanist-minded Italians, even by the greatest artist among them:

"Flemish painting," replied Michelangelo slowly, "will generally satisfy any devout person more than any Italian painting can. The latter will never make him shed a tear, whereas Flemish art will move him greatly, not through its force and excellence, but by reason of the virtues of the devout person himself. It is pleasing to women, those very old or very young in particular, and also to monks and nuns, and to some gentleman of breeding who, however, is insensible to the true harmony. In Flanders their one aim is to delude the eyes, painting things that are delightful in themselves or which no one dares deprecate, such as saints and prophets. Their pictures are made up of scraps of cloth, walls, green fields, clumps of trees, rivers, and bridges, the which they call landscapes, with many figures scattered here and there. All of that, even if to some it may appear beautiful, is, to tell the truth, painted without criteria or art, without symmetry or proportions, without taking pains in selecting what is to be shown though at the same time without spontaneity, and in short without substance or vigor."
FRANCISCO DE HOLLANDA, Da Pintura Antiga: Dialogos em Roma com Miguel Angelo, *1548.*

But this was special pleading on the part of a man who, even after he had proved his threefold genius in sculpture, painting, and architecture, continued to hold sculpture the highest art. His contemporaries thought otherwise:

Thinke you it againe a trifling matter to counterfeite naturall colours, flesh, cloth, and all other coloured thinges? This can not nowe the graver in marble doe, ne yet expresse the grace of the sight that is in the blacke eyes, or in azure with the shining of those amorous beames. Hee can not shew the colour of yellow haire, nor the glistring of armor, nor a darke night, nor a sea tempest, nor those twincklings and sparkes, nor the burning of a Citie, nor the rysing of the morning in the colour of Roses, with those beames of purple and golde. Finally hee can not shewe the skye, the sea, the earth, hilles, woodes, medowes, gardens, rivers, Cities, nor houses, which the Painter doth all. For this respect (me thinke) painting is more noble, and containeth in it a greater workmanship than graving in Marble.

BALDASSARE CASTIGLIONE, Il Libro del Cortegiano, *1528, translated by Sir Thomas Hoby, 1561.*

In Michelangelo's own time, Italian painting was making extraordinary strides in the conquest of the art of illusion, in deceiving the eye into taking the image for the truth. But Michelangelo's own stern Christian Neo-Platonism viewed with suspicion and distaste all attempts at trickery. What counted for him was the clear definition, the precise contour. For this reason he took a reactionary position and defended the old mediums of fresco and tempera against the new technique of painting with oils on canvas which Leonardo da Vinci and the Venetians, especially Titian, were using to create effects of atmosphere and sensuous textures:

I am told by men who spoke with Michelangelo that often that saintly old man used to weep, seeing that painting in tempera was going out of use, and that everyone was taking up oils, and he lamented that now true painting was over and done with. For myself, I dare to say that if they had not brought in this oil painting, we might have had fewer bad painters.

PABLO DE CESPEDES, Discurso de la comparación de la antigua y moderna pintura y escultura, *1604.*

Revolutionary as was Michelangelo's art, and that which he inspired in his followers, in one sense he was himself the last of the pioneers of the Renaissance and had lived on into an age of less lofty ideals. For him, man in his most ideal form, nude as his Creator made him, was still the center of the universe and the only worthy subject for art:

"The kind of painting that I so highly celebrate and praise," explained Michelangelo, "consists only in the imitation of any creature whatsoever that immortal God created with His great care and wisdom, and that He invented and painted in His own likeness, even to the beasts and birds, dispensing His perfection to each according to its merit. To my mind, that painting is excellent and divine which most resembles and best imitates any work whatsoever of the Eternal, be it a human figure, or a wild and strange animal, or a plain simple fish, or a bird in the sky, or whatever creature you wish. . . . It seems to me that to imitate perfectly each of these in its own species means nothing less than to desire to imitate the office of Eternal God. And, consequently, the most noble and excellent among works of art will be that in which has been copied the most noble of beings, the one who was created with the greatest refinement and science." FRANCISCO DE HOLLANDA, Dialogos em Roma...

But when man-the-artist set himself up as peer, and even rival, of God-the-Creator, then the way was open to an art which was not based on observation of nature and respect for the classical exemplars, but on man's inborn gift to imagine what does not, never did, never can, exist:

The divine character of painting is such that the spirit of the painter transforms itself into an image of the spirit of God, for, free in his power, he gives himself to the creation of divers species. . . . If the painter desires to behold beauties capable of inspiring in him love, he has the faculty of creating them. And if he wishes to see monstrous things which strike fear in the heart, or drolleries to excite laughter, or those things which arouse pity, he is their master and god. And if he wishes to create landscapes, deserts, shady cool places in the season of heat, he represents them, and also warm comforting places when the weather turns grim. If he would have valleys, if he desires to see vast panoramas from the high peaks of mountains, and if then he would behold the ocean's horizon, he has the power to do so. And if from the depths of valleys he would perceive high mountains, or from high mountains low-lying valleys or coasts, or whatever exists in the universe per esentia, presentia o imaginazione, *by essence, accident, or fiction, he has the power to do so, first in his mind and then in his hands. And his hands have such virtue that at a specific moment they can engender a harmony of proportions such that the eye conceives of it as reality itself.* LEONARDO DA VINCI, Codex Urbinas, lat. 1270, *Vatican Library, Rome.*

Whence two kinds of art came into being, not one as in the Quattrocento. Art became divided against itself:

Two sorts of imitation therefore exist: the Icastical and the Fantastical. The Icastical imitates things which are found in nature, the Fantastical those which have their existence only in the intellect of him who imitates.

GREGORIO COMANINI, Il Figino ovvero del fine della Pittura, *1591.*

Its unity lost, or destroyed, the Renaissance style was doomed to die. Beauty was no longer thought of as

Alberti's "harmony of all the parts... fitted together with such proportion and connection that nothing can be added, diminished, or altered." Artists made their own rules. For a Vasari, art was *grazia, facilità,* and *maniera*—elegant grace, the absence of signs of strain in the execution, and stylishness. Stylishness meant a fine style based not so much on observation of nature as on imitation of the best points of other artists' styles: Raphael's sweet elegance, Titian's color, Michelangelo's sublime *terribilità,* and the like—in short, their individual *manner.* But when one element of a style comes to preponderate, whatever it may be—form or color or expression or some other aspect in which an artist may find the one and only excellence of art—the pressure from within created by overemphasis on one element becomes too great to be controlled or contained, and the style explodes. It becomes something else, some new style with its own principles, its own logic or lack of logic. This is what happened around the third decade of the sixteenth century, when Raphael and Leonardo had died, and when Michelangelo created something entirely new in his tombs for the Medici. Abroad, as in Italy, men esteemed those three artists as the highest peaks that art had reached or could reach. Nothing remained but to carry forward the lessons they had taught. But the lessons were misunderstood, and what came into being was no longer Renaissance art but a new art which, more or less inappropriately, is called Mannerism. It was an art as diverse as the men who practiced it. For some it meant modish elegance, for others a strange transformation of reality into a dream or a nightmare, for still others a psychological exploration of man's soul, his relation to the things about him, to his own passions, and to good and evil—to the world, the flesh, and the devil. Its rules were drawn not from Nature or Antiquity but from each man's personal vision and experience.

So thoroughgoing was the change that it affected even such an abstract art as architecture. Fantasy was introduced into what had once been classical severity, functional propriety, and simple beauty. As the Early Renaissance understood it, pure geometrical forms existed in nature, and were therefore the most fitting and the most beautiful for men to imitate, whether in a painting, a building, or even an entire city. But Mannerist architects were unconcerned with such "natural geometry." They indulged in flights of fancy as extravagant as those of Mannerist painters and sculptors, and the external show of ingenious ornaments became of more moment than the functional simplicity of a building. It was against this self-indulgence and defiance of classical rules that Palladio reacted for aesthetic reasons:

What shall we say of that form of Building, which is so contrary to what Nature has taught us, that it deviates from that Simplicity which is visible in things here produc'd, and departs from all that is good, or true, or agreeable in the way of Building: for which reason, instead of Columns, or Pilasters, which are contriv'd to bear a great weight, one ought not to place those Modern Ornaments call'd Cartooshes, *which are certain* Scroles *that are but an eye-sore to the Artists, and give others only a confused Idea of* Architecture, *without any pleasure or satisfaction; nor indeed do they produce any other effect than to increase the Expences of the Builder.*

ANDREA PALLADIO, I quattro libri dell'Architettura, *1570, translated by Giacomo Leoni, 1715.*

In France, Philibert Delorme agreed heartily, and for very practical reasons:

But such ornaments must be made with great art and architectural majesty, and not with carved foliage, nor of delicate relief, since these merely attract filth, foulness, birds' nests, flies, and suchlike vermin. Further, such things are so fragile and so impermanent, that when they begin to fall into ruin, instead of giving pleasure, they give the greatest displeasure and make a sad spectacle accompanied by much annoyance. I call all of that money down the drain, except that it serve as a melancholy spite against the future.

PHILIBERT DELORME, Le Premier tome de l'Architecture, *1567.*

But Reason itself played less and less of a role. With new techniques of painting in oils or modeling in stucco which created an ever more perfect illusion, with the new virtuosity in rendering anatomy, the senses more and more took over. The high moral aims of the Early Renaissance were forgotten, in religious art as much as in profane. In Dürer's time, it was still necessary to defend the reawakened pagan gods by speaking of them as if they were precursors of the Christian heroes:

> *Just as the Ancients attributed to their false god Apollo the most beautiful traits of a man, so do we wish to employ the same measures for Christ our Lord, but in chastity. And as they showed Venus as the most beautiful of women, so too—but chastely—do we aspire to portray the most pure Virgin Mary. And their Hercules will we transform into our Samson, and so with all the rest of the gods.*
>
> ALBRECHT DÜRER, *preliminary draft for* Vier Bücher von menschlicher Proportion, *1528.*

By the middle of the sixteenth century, first in Italy, then throughout Europe, and most of all at the royal courts of Fontainebleau and Prague, the man within the god—or, to be more precise, the woman—was finally released. Apollo, Hercules, and, most of all, Venus became objects of sensual delight, having cast off, along with the last scraps of their clothing, all vestiges of the classical and Christian dignity the Humanists had conferred on them. The nude figure was conceived as an object of beauty in itself, raw material to be kneaded, molded, twisted into the most exciting of shapes:

> *It is reported then that* Michaell Angelo *upon a time gave this observation to the Painter* Marcus de Sciena *his scholler: that he should alwaies make a figure* Pyramidall, Serpentlike, *and multiplied by one, two and three. In which precept (in mine opinion) the whole mysterie of the arte consisteth. For the greatest grace and life, that a picture can have, is, that it expresse* Motion: *which the Painters call the* spirite *of a picture. Nowe there is no forme so fitte to expresse this* motion *as that of the flame of fire . . . for it hath a* Conus *or sharpe pointe wherewith it seemeth to divide the aire, that so it may ascende to his proper sphere. . . . Now this is to bee understoode after two sortes: either that the* Conus *of the* Pyramis *bee placed upwardes and the* base *downe-wardes, as in the fier; or else contrary wise, with the* base *upwardes and the* Conus *downe-wardes. In the first it expresseth the width and largeness of a picture, about the legges and garmentes belowe; shewing it slender above* Pyramidall-wise, *by discovering one shoulder and hiding the other, which is shortened by the turning of the body. In the seconde, it sheweth the figure biggest in the upper partes; by representing either both the shoulders, or both the armes, shewing one legge and hiding the other, or both of them after one sorte, as the skillfull Painter shall judge fittest for his purpose. So that his meaning is, that it shoulde resemble the forme of the letter* S *placed right, or else turned the wronge way as* S; *because then it hath his beauty.*
>
> GIOVANNI PAOLO LOMAZZO, Trattato dell'Arte della Pittura, *1584, translated by Richard Haydock, 1598.*

This flamelike form, the *figura serpentinata*, represents one aspect of Mannerism, its devious play with natural forms to astound and delight the viewer. This new geometry, non-Euclidean so to speak, became the common property of all Mannerist artists as much as the circle, square, and triangle had been for those of the Renaissance.

There was also another, and darker, side to Mannerism. At the start of the Renaissance, the artist was no more than a member of a craft guild. By his own achievements, he rose in the social scale so high that, even when not ennobled by some admiring monarch, he might live "more like a prince than a painter, with numerous horses and servants, his house furnished with tapestries, silver, and other valuable furniture," which was Rosso's style of life at Fontainebleau if we can trust Vasari. With success came arrogance, the certainty that a single work of art was a surer guaranty of immortality than all the deeds of kings and popes.

But the sense of personal greatness brought with it eccentricity. Vasari himself recognized this: Rosso died a suicide in the midst of his tapestries and silver, Parmigianino "doted on his alchemy, overpowered by its infatuation, allowed his beard to grow long and disordered, which made him look like a savage instead of a gentleman. He neglected himself and grew melancholy and eccentric." Pontormo "had strange notions, and was so fearful of death that he never allowed it to be mentioned, and he avoided dead bodies. He never went to feasts or to other places where crowds collected for fear of being crushed, and he was solitary beyond belief." This was the other face of Mannerism, the one that turned inward, tortured by personal anguish or Christian guilt in the years when Reform and Counter Reform harrowed men's minds with doubts; and this too showed itself in art, in morbid introspection or religious ecstasy:

We come now to discourse of painters with a melancholy, saturnine temperament, wrathful and ill-disposed. In the works of such a man, though his intent may be to paint angels and saints, his natural disposition leads him, in whatever he may strive to imitate, to paint almost without realizing it things which are terrible and disordered beyond anyone's power to imagine save his own. FELIPE DE GUEVARA, Comentarios...

When imagination rules, the laws derived from Nature and Reason must be suspended, along with the moral precepts of tradition. Alberti and Piero della Francesca, Leonardo and Dürer were left far behind, and their lessons fell on deaf ears when Mannerism reached its climax:

But I insist, and know I speak the truth, that the art of painting neither derives its principles from, nor has any need to consult, the mathematical sciences in order to learn rules and methods for what it does, nor even for its theoretical speculations. Because art is not the daughter of those sciences but of Nature and Design. One shows her the forms, the other teaches her what must be done. And thus the painter, once he has learned the first lessons and basic skills from his predecessors, or from Nature herself, becomes valorous in his art through his own natural inborn judgment together with careful diligence and observation of the beautiful and the good, without further help from or need for mathematics. FEDERICO ZUCCARI, L'Idea de' scultori, pittori e architetti, *1607.*

The concern of Mannerist art was, therefore, the appearances of things as the intellect, the imagination, and the human passion of the artist would have them be, not as they are:

This is the true, the proper, the universal end of painting: to be the imitator of Nature and also of all those artificial things that delude and deceive the eyes of living men and of the wisest among them. And beyond this, it gives expression to the gestures, motions, movements of life as seen in the eyes, mouth, hands which, portrayed exactly as they are, reveal the inward passions, love, hate, desire, impetuosity, delight, bliss, sadness, pain, hope, despair, fear, audacity, rage, reasoning, teaching, disputing, willing, commanding, obeying, and, in brief, all human acts and feelings. FEDERICO ZUCCARI, L'Idea...

Beyond this, art could not, would not, go. When Zuccari wrote this, Agostino Carracci was already dead, his brother Annibale soon would be, and the young Caravaggio had only three more years ahead of him. Rubens had just turned thirty, Bernini and Poussin were boys still, but a new style had already been born. Mannerist fantasy and unreason were doomed by the very intensity with which they were expressed. Their place would be taken by that new conception of order and reason which is called the Baroque.

Not all of anyone's favorite artists and works of art will be found here, not even the authors'. Some great men have been given small place and some, in fact, neglected. Lesser men have been perhaps made to seem greater than they were. The aim has been not to tell again the often-told story of persons and places but, much more, the less often considered, yet no less fascinating, story of how forms were born, throve, and were transformed into or replaced by new forms, how an art that grew up in the trusting world of the Renaissance steered a perilous way through events that changed men's thoughts and ways of living and became the very different, but no less significant, art of Mannerism.

Filippo Brunelleschi (1377–1446). The Sacrifice of Isaac. 1402. Gilded bronze relief, 18^1/$_8$ × 15^3/$_4$″. National Museum of the Bargello, Florence.

Cities, like men, have their years of pride when ambition is bridled only by the power of the imagination. To realize its dream of becoming the new Athens, Florence at the start of the Quattrocento had creative genius and wealth in a measure known to few other cities in history. As a first step, it set about enriching and—the word is significant—modernizing its ancient octagonal Baptistery. In 1401 the Merchants' Guild launched a competition for designs for a new bronze door for that edifice. The victor was the goldsmith Ghiberti who collected and studied Greek and Roman statues and who later wrote an autobiography in which he surveyed the history of art leading up to his own time.

Of the models submitted to the competition, two have survived. Their external form is the same Gothic quatrefoil used by Andrea Pisano in the 1330s for the other door already in place. But in seventy years much had changed. By 1401 man was making of himself the center of his own world. A world which, for Ghiberti, had balance, a fragile poise, a goldsmith's elegance not too unlike that of the last years of the Gothic. For Brunelleschi, his rival, it was the new scene of a drama involving man. And yet both harked back to what, for them, was a fabulous past: Ghiberti's Isaac is modeled after a second-century B.C. Greek torso he owned; Brunelleschi's relief includes a figure that recalls the Roman statue of a boy pulling a thorn from his foot.

Lorenzo Ghiberti (1378–1455). The Sacrifice of Isaac. 1402. Gilded bronze relief, 18^1/$_2$ × 17^3/$_8$″. National Museum of the Bargello, Florence.

Twenty-three years later Ghiberti began work on the East Door, and by then the "rebirth" meant more than the revival of Antique motifs. With a sure architectonic sense, he simplified the design from twenty-eight to ten rectangular relief panels enclosed in a framework where Old Testament prophets and sibyls, in typically Renaissance shell-vaulted niches, alternate with heads (Ghiberti's own portrait among them) in roundels, the whole linked by arabesques of foliage and closed off, above and below, by oval medallions with reclining Antique river-gods. But it was in the reliefs themselves that the Renaissance triumphed. Ghiberti proclaimed, "Proportion alone makes beauty," and his classically proportioned figures are placed in settings which, however grandiose, are of the measure of man; complex and agitated as the scenes may be, everything in them works in harmony. From high relief in the foreground down to the very low relief in the seemingly far distance, all is governed by the laws of perspective. This, then, is a central principle of the Renaissance: to create a world, and an art, in which man can move with naturalness in the space about him, in his natural—no longer symbolic—environment.

◄ Lorenzo Ghiberti. The "Doors of Paradise." 1425–52. Gilded bronze, 15′ × 8′3″. Baptistery, Florence.

Lorenzo Ghiberti. The Story of Joseph, detail of the "Doors of Paradise." 1425–52. Gilded bronze relief, 31¼″ square. Baptistery, Florence.

Gothic space had been irrational—an arbitrary rule-of-thumb definition in paintings, a problem scarcely faced up to in statues, a measureless yearning in cathedrals. It could be magical or inspiring, but it could never appear logical to the human mind which desires things as they are, or seem to be. Mysticism was not the prerogative of the Gothic; the Renaissance was fully as mystical, but its divinity was expressed in the orderliness, the rightness, of the square, oblong, cube, triangle, and circle. With the simplest of geometry, Brunelleschi explored that mystery and found it to be nothing but the way we rationalize the space around us, the rules of sight, and this meant linear perspective, the apparent tendency of all parallel lines to converge in a single distant vanishing point, a principle applying equally well to architecture, painting, sculpture, and even city planning. In his design for San Lorenzo, Brunelleschi introduced other new principles. In accord with Renaissance mysticism which held that divine harmony was present in all things, from man's soul to the body politic to the ordered movement of the spheres and seasons, he "tuned" his building to a single module—the surface area of the transept—which he repeated four times in the nave, once in the choir (in his reliefs Ghiberti did likewise, a single square of the foreground pavement serving as a module for the height of the figures as well as for the over-all dimensions). Even more opposed to the Gothic was another innovation: where the older architecture had striven to conceal the weight and thrust of its members by an infinite soaring verti-

cality, Brunelleschi—engineer as well as architect—let it be clearly seen that the slender Corinthian columns, fluted pilasters, and elegant cornices which he imitated from Antique models bear all the weight of the semicircular arches and the coffered flat ceiling. Thus, in San Lorenzo clarity reigns over all: in the simple orderliness of its ground plan, in the honesty of its engineering, in the unadorned rightness of its members, in the harmonious proportions of all its relationships. These were lessons Brunelleschi had learned firsthand from the ruins of ancient Rome. But all Rome was not in Rome. The Early Renaissance made a naïve but profitable mistake: it took as authentically ancient the Romanesque churches of the eleventh century and earlier which stood in Florence (the Baptistery, San Miniato, Santi Apostoli), and these provided other models of simplicity and order. All these lessons, though, might have led to sterile imitation had it not been for the creative originality and clear-minded intelligence of the Renaissance. No Roman temple looked like San Lorenzo, nor any Gothic cathedral. Those may stir the soul; a Renaissance church confers peace on the mind.

The lesson was not lost on painting. Masaccio's *Trinity*, whose architecture imitates Brunelleschi's or may even have been designed by him, creates the illusion of a finite depth in which the six figures all have a normal man's height, unlike Gothic painting where divine beings are supernaturally immense, saints only less so, and humans reduced to the lowliest dimensions their pride could bear.

It is certain that not everything in the Renaissance came about through imitation of Antiquity. Masaccio's figures are blocklike, sculpturesque, massive, something unseen since Giotto's death almost a century before, and the young Masaccio must have studied the long-dead master's frescoes. But Giotto's figures were immobile—monuments through all eternity—and those of the Gothic artists after him were slender ghosts quivering at the slightest breath of reality. Masaccio's move, and of their own volition. Beneath their painted draperies, muscle and bone prepare to take the next step forward, and their feet conform to Vasari's criterion of "modernity": they do not perch on tiptoe as in Gothic paintings but stand firmly on the ground, flat and foreshortened. Further, their volumes are modeled by light which flows from the right in the painting and coincides with the natural light from the chapel window. What is more, Masaccio's figures are masters of the space they move in. Behind them bare hills stretch to a distant horizon, hills solid and real enough to be climbed, their recession into the distance ingeniously marked by the perspective lines of a few trees. It is a

Masaccio. The Tribute Money, from the cycle The Acts of Saint Peter. c. 1424–28. Fresco, 8'4³/₈" × 19'7³/₈". Brancacci Chapel, Santa Maria del Carmine, Florence.

world in which a complex action can unfold realistically, not merely symbolically as in Gothic art where each small episode of a narration is confined to a separate frame or jumbled together without logic of time and place. Here, in the center, the tax collector demands his tribute money and Christ commands Peter to seek for the coin in the mouth of a fish. At the left, Peter draws a fish out of the lake, at the right he delivers the coin to the guardian of the gate. The four actions appear before us simultaneously, but so credible are the personages and their environment that we "read" them as phases of a single action. By means of science—the techniques of rendering perspective, anatomy, movement, light, and facial expression—a minor miracle of Our Lord is raised here to a major miracle of art. We *believe* Masaccio's painting, we accept as true that this is the way human beings look and act in a real world. That was the goal and achievement of Renaissance painting and of its earliest master: "The things made before his time may be termed merely paintings; by comparison, his creations are real, living, and natural" (Vasari).

The central problem facing artists at the beginning of the fifteenth century was how to break away from the stereotyped formulas which had for so long dominated all of the arts. Giotto had tried to shake off Byzantine rigidity, had made an attempt to place convincingly round figures in a credible space, and to confer some semblance of humanity on them by giving them movements and gestures in which we can recognize our own. But the men who followed Giotto were of a lesser breed, or conceived their task in a different fashion. By the end of the fourteenth century, a single Gothic style prevailed throughout Europe. Female figures were willowy, male figures spindly, settings arbitrary and fantastic. Pictures were stuffed with great numbers of supernumerary figures or irrelevant chunks of architecture to symbolize a pictorial space which did not, in fact, exist. With such a *horror vacui*, harmony and unity were ruled out, a balanced rhythmic composition was impossible, expressiveness could reside in the detail only, never in the whole. Meaning was therefore secondhand, symbolic, never direct and immediate. The significance of the Renaissance revolt against this abstractness lies not in the discovery of certain technical-scientific devices to give the illusion of round bodies in deep space on the plane surface of a picture but, rather, in the end for which those discoveries were used: to create a simulacrum of reality in which men could recognize themselves and their environment, not as symbols but as the fact itself. And that "realness" made the "message" of the work of art more pungent. For this, the most useful means was the representation of things as they are, in their natural forms. The tools available were study of the nude and of plants and animals from life, linear perspective, foreshortening, plus one other—the imitation of Antiquity, its art, and its ideas. Pagan man was the naked natural creature of a time before

Paolo Uccello (1397–1475). The Battle of San Romano. c. 1455. Panel, 5'11⅝" × 10'7⅛". The Uffizi, Florence.

Paolo Uccello. The Hunt. After 1460. Panel, $25^5/_8 \times 65''$. Ashmolean Museum, Oxford.

the Fall, and so Antiquity and Nature were one and the same, the uncorrupted essence of man and man's world. To return to Antiquity was to return to Nature, and both led back to Man. Neither was an end in itself, but only an aid to the artist in communicating whatever it was—whether sacred or profane did not matter—that he wished to communicate.

Not all Renaissance artists sought the "natural" as we understand it. "Crazy Paolo," as Uccello was called by his contemporaries, was not obsessed with nature as such but with the geometry which lies hidden within natural forms (his wife complained that he preferred his "sweet perspective" to her charms). "Solitary, eccentric, melancholy, and poor"—the words are Vasari's—"he was always attracted by the most difficult things in art." Reality, for him, lay in geometrical form, not natural color, and to bring this out, to Vasari's horror, "he made his fields blue, his city red, his buildings of various hues according to his fancy." In his *Battle of San Romano*, one of three done for the Medici's palace, a close examination reveals the hundreds of objects, men, and horses scattered about the field, each a dazzling abstract study in stereometry, in perspective foreshortening. Lances, crossbows, banners create a thicket of perspective lines. Men and horses, afoot or dead, make a patchwork of stereometric volumes seen from the most impossible angles, all of it in what Vasari termed a "dry, sharp style." In the hunting scene, the style is even drier, and the first impression is of a late-medieval tapestry with ornamental puppetlike figures set against a landscape without depth. It belongs, in fact, to the decorative arts, since it was the panel or lid of a *cassone*, a storage chest. But the flowers and bushes in the foreground lead the eye back cleverly—scientifically—to the wraiths of trees which form regular series of arcades like those used by more conventional Renaissance painters to convey an impression of three-dimensional depth. Fantasy world as it may be, Uccello's is no less real than Masaccio's, and no less true to the Renaissance idea that perfect order as set down by the scientist-artist is superior to the mere accident of nature that anyone can see.

Andrea del Castagno (1423–57). Saint Julian and the Redeemer. c. 1454/55. Detached fresco, $81^7/_8 \times 70^7/_8$". Santissima Annunziata, Florence.

Domenico Veneziano (c. 1410–61). ▶ Madonna and Child with Saints. c. 1445. Panel, $6'7^1/_2$" × $6'11^7/_8$". The Uffizi, Florence.

Another of Vasari's eccentrics was the "vile" Andrea del Castagno—"inhuman, inferior to the brutes, unworthy to live." He did not, *pace* Vasari, murder out of envy his friend Domenico Veneziano one serenading evening by "smashing both his lute and his stomach with some lead": Domenico survived Andrea by four years. Yet, writing a century later, Vasari may well have been led to this cock-and-bull story by what he sensed in Castagno's art. There is, indeed, something brooding and intense in it, a somber anguish, as in this fresco of the murderer-saint Julian listening with vibrant tension—look at the hands—to the voice of the Redeemer. Always with Castagno there is a sense of immediate presence, of the dramatic moment, and this came not from Masaccio's monumentality but, rather, from Andrea's own bold style of drawing and from the vigorous movement of Donatello's sculpture. Henceforth Florentine art was to gravitate between two poles: the linearity of drawing as against the sense of mass in movement great sculpture gives. Color would be only an adjunct, never the central factor.

In the first generation of the Florentine Renaissance, color and light were used only as aids in modeling statuesque figures. Then as later, color and light belonged to Venice, not to Florence. In 1438 a little-known painter of Venetian origin offered his services to Piero de' Medici, proposing to equal—at least—the achievements of the most admired local painters, Fra Angelico and Filippo Lippi. If Domenico Veneziano learned the new art of perspective from Florence, what he brought there was a feeling for the freshness of daylight, a morning-clearness which, in fact, is the light of Florence itself, but which, oddly enough, its own painters

had not as yet perceived. So beautifully did Domenico harmonize two opposite conceptions that he was able to use light to articulate a composition (note how the triangular shadow seals the Madonna and Child into their niche) and to bind into a unity all the separate shapes and colors—the blond flesh and pastel garments of the figures, the delicately molded forms of the marble architecture, the green and orange of the fruit trees against a Mediterranean-blue sky. Domenico exerted a lasting influence, and not least in what he taught his young assistant from southern Tuscany, Piero della Francesca.

Naturalness was the conscious goal of the Renaissance. Its higher goal was purely aesthetic: to invent a coherent, rational order for life and art, to impose logic on the accidental. Not "realistic," Piero della Francesca's art renounces all unnecessary and superfluous acts and objects of human life. True, his figures seem human: even angels are without wings or halos and stand peasant-solid on the ground. Yet we never question that they *are* angels, because an unheard music flows through pictures which are as undisturbed, as right, as the Divine Order. Human or divine, the personages can never move of their free will, as can Masaccio's Apostles, lest the pictorial order be shattered. They are art, not life: perfect abstractions. The Queen will never rise, the shepherd never cease to direct our eye to the central vanishing point, the hand on the lute never sound the next chord.

Piero della Francesca (c. 1410/20–92). The Nativity. c. 1470–75. Panel, 49 × 48¹/₂″. National Gallery, London.

Piero della Francesca. The Queen of Sheba Adores the Bridge from Which ▶ the Cross Will Be Made, detail of the cycle The Story of the True Cross. c. 1455. Fresco, entire scene 11′ × 24′6¹/₈″. San Francesco, Arezzo.

Not everyone, not even in Florence, shared the same goal, nor wished to. The simple monk who came to be known as the Blessed Angelico felt no urge to explore a new world. As a Dominican, his single task was to preach the Word that had always been. Tempted for a time by the discoveries of Masaccio, he took from them only a clearer organization of composition—which helped his preaching by making the narrative easier to follow—and a certain sense of mass in his figures. But though his figures seem tangible and have volume, they have no weight, because the space in which they move is not quite real, is closer to fable than to fact. Even when he attempts perspective, there is no true depth but only a doll's-house space for his doll-like figures. He was not alone in resisting the new art. In Siena, a day's muleback-ride from Florence, Gothic traits lingered on, still exquisite in the mysticism of an earlier time, adding no more than a touch of perspective, a hint of firmer composition, an Antique motif here and there.

Renaissance pictures were perfect rectangles, the perspective within them made perfect triangles, churches and palaces were shaped into perfect cubes. This aesthetic geometry was completed by the most perfect form of all, the circle. The *tondo* appeared everywhere: the round painting became a new form especially appropriate for scenes of the childhood of Christ, round medallions complemented and enhanced the sterner vertical and horizontal architecture of chapels and sacristies, relief sculptors found that round plaques lent an even greater illusion of depth, and the workshop of the Della Robbia family turned out thousands of brightly

colored glazed terra-cotta garlands encircling emblems of the Guilds, heraldic mottoes, or Madonnas as splendid, gay decoration for public places and private homes.

Whatever the subject, the Della Robbia ceramics became immensely popular with all strata of the population, the perfect expression of the optimistic delight in the here-and-now, in the object beautiful for its own sake; and this was typical of an age that thought of its dwellings and its cities in terms of aesthetics as well as of comfort.

▲
Filippo Lippi (c. 1406–69). Madonna and Child, with Stories of the Virgin and Saint Anne in the Background. 1452. Panel, diameter 53^1/$_8$". Palatine Gallery, Palazzo Pitti, Florence.

◀ Fra Angelico (1387?–1455). The Martyrdom of Saints Cosmas and Damian. c. 1445/50. Predella panel from the former high altar of San Marco, 14^5/$_8$ × 18^1/$_8$". National Gallery of Ireland, Dublin.

Luca della Robbia (1399–1482). Madonna of the Flower Hedge. Glazed terra cotta, 32^5/$_8$ × 25". National Museum of the Bargello, Florence.

Unknown Urbino Artist. View of an Ideal City. c. 1475. Panel, 23⁵/₈ × 78³/₄″. Palazzo Ducale, Urbino.

Not that the Renaissance was indifferent to the Heavenly City—that is a nineteenth-century notion long exploded. But it felt that, itself, it could do more toward improving the City of Man. True to its ideal and aim, this meant imposing order on an urban agglomeration which might otherwise be disordered and hence not only inefficient but also unaesthetic. City plans became geometrical, classical, as much a work of art as is this other ideal city realized in paint, itself an exemplary illustration of linear perspective (note how the houses diminish in size with distance) as well as of the round church, a form the Renaissance considered ideal both aesthetically and spiritually.

The buildings constructed, and not merely dreamed of, were also art, though the greatest single construction of the age, the cupola of the Duomo in Florence, did not truly belong to the Renaissance. Its conception as a double shell went back to 1367, and when Brunelleschi became Master of Works in 1420 he had to swear not to alter that plan. The Renaissance cupola is often a hemisphere, like its Roman ancestors, but here the separate segments resemble Gothic pointed arches and rise steeply to form a kind of cloister vault. The problem Brunelleschi faced concerned not architecture as such but engineering, and there he proved his genius. For the first time in history a dome rose to immense height unsupported by a wooden armature and with inner and outer shells of bricks retaining the same thickness throughout, no matter how steep the curvature became. The result was a dome of not excessive weight, structurally stable and aesthetically satisfying, "immense enough," Alberti said, "to cover with its shade all the population of Tuscany" and, he added, probably surpassing the skill of the Ancients.

Alberti himself was a scholar, author of great books on architecture and painting, who did not necessarily execute his own plans. Going beyond Ghiberti's definition, he defined Beauty as "a harmony of all the parts... fitted together with such proportion and connection that nothing can be added, diminished, or altered." His Rucellai Palace is a tightly, perfectly joined union of all its elements: the three classical orders of pilasters are superimposed on a flat but textured—"rusticated"—wall, and they both separate and link the semi-

Filippo Brunelleschi. Cupola of the Cathedral, Florence. 1420–36.
Height 298′6″, diameter 149′4″.

Leon Battista Alberti (1404–72) and Bernardo Rossellino (1409–64)
Palazzo Rucellai, Florence. 1446–51.

circular-arched bilobate windows. Nothing is in excess: the
verticality of the pilasters is balanced by horizontal cornices,
and gently but firmly closed off at the top by a crowning
cornice. All Gothic striving has been eliminated; what remains
is a sensitively balanced perfect cube.

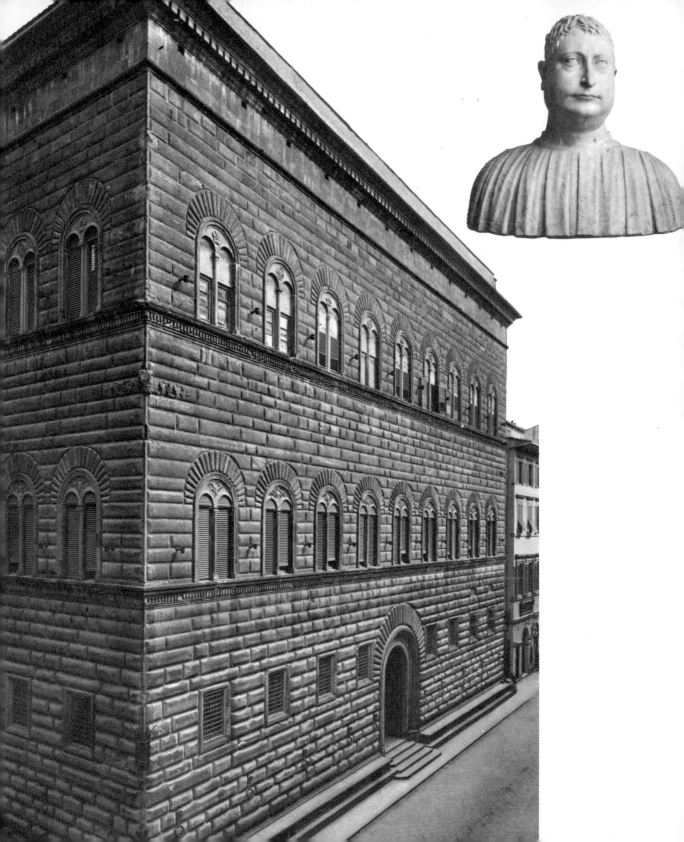

Florence was ruled by powerful patrician merchants. It had never toyed with the overrefined, fantastic game of chivalry played in the small courts in the International Gothic period, and once the first flush of the Early Renaissance was over, Florence's way of life was based on solid industry, high finance, intellectual seriousness, and moral discipline. For its palaces, Brunelleschi's serenity and the erudite grace of Alberti soon came to be considered too intimate a face to present to public view. Patrician dwellings became monumental, massive piles of rough-hewn rusticated stone with no more than the graceful windows of the upper stories as purely functional decoration. Behind the heavy but beautifully proportioned walls, though, the private life of public figures took place in large airy rooms around a central courtyard surrounded by classical arcades and open to the sun. The top floor was usually an open loggia, a Renaissance innovation typical of a more comfortable manner of living in which light and air had become as necessary as food.

To escape from the city, there were villas in the nearby countryside. How much the age owed to the spirit of classical Antiquity, how little to its letter, is seen in this country house built for Lorenzo the Magnificent. True, it is set on a podium like a Roman temple, but the podium has become an arcaded ground floor for utility rooms. A miniature Ionic temple appears on the first floor, but it is only an entrance portico reached by a sweeping double staircase and scarcely projects from the flat whitewashed wall behind it. But most of all, the building is exactly what it was meant to be, a gracious retreat for a Renaissance poet-statesman, set on a hill amid parks and gardens and herb plots.

▲
Mino da Fiesole (c. 1430–84). Niccolò Strozzi. 1454. Marble, height 19$^1/_4$". State Museums, Berlin-Dahlem.

◀ Benedetto da Maiano (1442–97) and Simone del Pollaiolo called Il Cronaca (1457–1508). Palazzo Strozzi, Florence. Begun 1489, continued 1497–1507.

Giuliano da Sangallo (1445–1516). Villa Medicea, Poggio a Caiano, vicinity of Florence. 1480–85.

A gentler way of life called for finely carved and inlaid furniture, rich tapestry hangings, elegant table service. The glazed, tin-enameled earthenware known as "majolica" (probably from the Hispano-Moresque ceramics of Majorca) first appeared in Italy around 1420 and was soon turned out in Urbino, Casteldurante, Faenza (whence "faïence"), and Cafaggiolo, the latter the site of a villa built for Cosimo de' Medici the Elder who gave his patronage to the local artisans in ceramic. From the outset, the designs were taken from the rich repertory of mythological imagery that the Renaissance Humanists had rediscovered.

Majolica plate. c. 1515. Cafaggiolo-ware, diameter 15½″. Victoria and Albert Museum, London.

Leon Battista Alberti. San Francesco (the "Tempio Malatestiano"), Rimini. Exterior designed 1450.

Rimini on the Adriatic coast was ruled by a benevolent, cultured, art-loving despot, Sigismondo Malatesta. As a funeral monument for himself and his consort, he chose to have the old church of San Francesco remodeled by Alberti into something more akin to his Humanist spirit. For the façade, Alberti borrowed the basic forms of the triumphal arch of Emperor Augustus in Rimini—pagan forms for a Christian temple, a true Renaissance conception. Corinthian fluted half-columns, pilasters, semicircular arches, round medallions, a triangular pediment—here is the repertory of Antique forms taken over by the Renaissance. On the flanks were deep barrel-vaulted niches, those on the south with classical sarcophaguses for the remains of the scholars Sigismondo had gathered around him, plus those of the great Greek mystic Gemistus Pletho which Sigismondo brought back as both booty and relic from his campaigns in the East. Sigismondo died; his sepulcher was never finished. Had it been, Alberti planned to complete the façade with curving half-gables at either side, the volute-motif destined to develop throughout the Renaissance and Baroque.

Andrea Bregno (1418–1503) and Donato Bramante (1444–1514). Palazzo Riario (Cancelleria), Rome. 1483–1517.

For Mantua, Alberti designed a church which speaks the language of Imperial Rome even more impressively. The triumphal-arch motif of its façade is carried indoors to make a grandiose rhythmic procession of barrel-vaulted arches over the side chapels. A single vast nave lies open to the light, uninterrupted by columns or pillars (compare Brunelleschi's San Lorenzo). Gigantic flat pilasters rise to either side of the chapels, supporting a delicate cornice surmounted by the immense coffered barrel vault over the nave. Grace and grandeur are combined here as nowhere else.

A quarter-century later, Rome, a shabby ruin in the early Quattrocento, was rebuilding its past glory in the forms of the Renaissance. Though the Cancelleria derives from the Palazzo Rucellai in Florence, it enlarges the span and height of that building, gives a forceful rhythm to the alternation of pilasters and windows, imposes a more emphatic horizontal accent on the three stories and the upper cornice. Nothing is left undefined: the corner bays project slightly to make it clear that there the building ends. Rome's art and architecture were to be always on the scale of its past glory and present power.

Luciano Laurana (c. 1420–79). Main court, Palazzo Ducale, Urbino. 1465–72 (top story added later). ►

Leon Battista Alberti. Interior, Sant' Andrea, Mantua. Designed 1472, completed around 1494; decoration and cupola of the 16th and 17th centuries.

Most civilized of courts and cities was Urbino. Perched on a tall crag rising clear of the wooded slopes, it lived in refined isolation, menaced only now and again by the land-hungry Papal States. Between threats and incursions, the days passed in sports and study, the evenings in music and intelligent talk (in the Ducal Palace took place the conversations reported by Baldassare Castiglione in the most civilized book ever written, *The Courtier*). For the palace, Laurana designed a broad, sunny inner court surrounded by graceful arcades above which the second story is articulated rhythmically in the vertical plane by smooth flat pilasters, in the horizontal by inscriptions in Humanist Roman letters eulogizing Federigo da Montefeltro, Duke of Urbino.

Baccio Pontelli (c. 1450–92). Studiolo, Palazzo Ducale, Urbino. 1477–82.

Indoors, the spacious rooms are decorated with a wealth of marble and stucco reliefs, their subjects drawn from mythology and Neo-Platonic symbolism. The gem of the palace is the *studiolo*, the Duke's private study—a tiny room with walls completely covered by inlaid wood panels which give the illusion of being cupboards crammed with books, musical instruments, astrolabes, hourglasses, and armor (Federigo was, after all, a soldier also). Never before had marquetry work been done with such virtuosity, nor perspective exploited with such skill as to make objects seem so believably three-dimensional. A worthy study room for the same Duke who built two tiny chapels side by side, one dedicated to the Holy Ghost, the other to the Muses, and who gave his patronage to Piero della Francesca, not only a painter but also the author of a treatise on perspective, the science of which he was a master, and to the mathematician Luca Pacioli.

For the palace, Piero painted a double portrait of the Duke and his wife Battista Sforza. Though the artist had long since solved the problem of the face in three-quarter profile, here he chose to use the traditional, heraldic full profile as found on Antique coins and medals. But there is nothing archaic about these portraits. It is as if Piero had ripped away the neutral dark background always used for portraits before his and revealed, as if for the first time, the light and sun and the moisture of rivers condensing in air and the green and brown of the earth on which men live. An ideal world, perhaps, but one so real that wisps of haze hang in the pockets of valleys, and colors and shapes pale in the vague far distance. And this was something no one before Piero had thought of and done. Not until Leonardo da Vinci would such effects of *sfumato*, of haze and light in

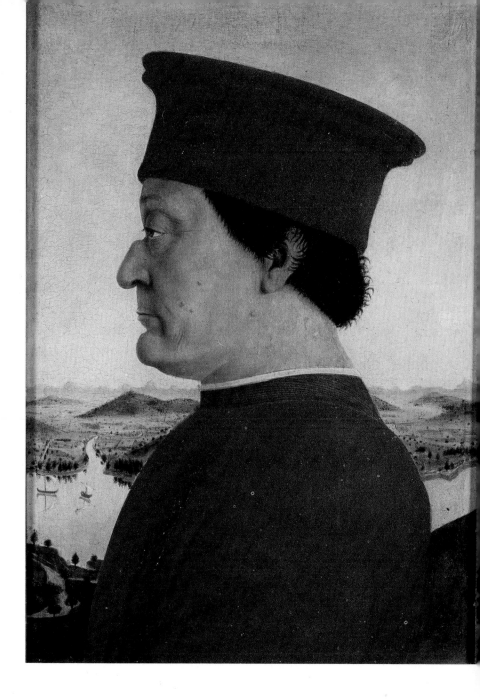

Piero della Francesca. Portrait of Federigo da Montefeltro, Duke of Urbino. c. 1465. Panel, 18$\frac{1}{2}$ × 13″. The Uffizi, Florence.

the distance, be achieved again. Did Piero learn this from the Flemish artists at Federigo's court, Justus of Ghent for one? So it is said, but no Fleming, not even Van Eyck, had ever "portrayed" a landscape with such a sense of the feel of sun and dew on the skin, of the smell of meadows and woods. And in contrast to multiform nature, Federigo himself is a great solid volume in a transparent atmosphere, and his eye and nose and chin are clear geometrical forms.

Sandro Botticelli (1444/45–1510). Madonna of the Magnificat. c. 1482. Panel, diameter 45¹/₄″. The Uffizi, Florence.

In Medicean Florence, Botticelli's approach to reality was an intellectual one. His creatures are perfect, no wrinkle in face or garment betrays their humanity, they are infinitely poised, almost intolerably beautiful. Their bodies are weightless; even Mars is a lithe youth, not a muscle-bound warrior. The figures are as if in low relief, not lacking in volume but really more drawing than painting. Limpid in atmosphere, transparent, sensuous but not sensual, Botticelli's art is the perfect expression of the Neo-Platonism which had reigned unchallenged in Florence ever since Cosimo de' Medici the Elder had founded the Platonic Academy. It was there that his grandson Lorenzo the Magnificent, poet as well as statesman, learned the higher ideal which, for a time, made Florence the intellectual, spiritual, and artistic capital of the Renaissance world.

Sandro Botticelli. Venus and Mars. c. 1483. Panel, $27^{1}/_{4} \times 68^{1}/_{4}''$. National Gallery, London.

In that ideal—so soon to be shattered by Savonarola after Lorenzo's premature death in 1492—there was no contradiction between spirit and flesh, between Christianity and pagan Antiquity. All were reconciled in the Godhead that was before time: Plato and Moses alike announced the Coming. The thought was fundamentally Christian, but the forms in which it was expressed could be pagan. Mary and Venus were as one, and the canticle of praise, the *Magnificat anima mea*, that the angels and Madonna read in Botticelli's *tondo* could be intoned also by the nude Celestial Venus rising from the waves in his *Birth of Venus* and by the bridelike Earthly Venus of his *Primavera*. For Venus had two natures, human and divine, in the thought of Marsilio Ficino, Florence's Neo-Platonic mentor. Like the Virgin, she was both Woman and Principle. Nude, she was divine, the pure Idea revealed to the philosopher; clothed, she was human, the moral, ethical principle by which men live, or should live. To the Renaissance, nudity was not licentious: the nude Celestial Venus is chaste and, at the same time, all-fecundating. Love is of the spirit as well as the senses, Ficino said. Beauty is born of God and draws men to Him, Love passes through the world and exalts it, and Pleasure returns to its Author and unites Him to His work. Thus a perfect circle from God to God is formed, which explains why the *tondo*, the circular picture, was a favorite of the Renaissance, not merely as an aesthetically pleasing form but also as a symbol of divine love and therefore particularly appropriate to pictures of the Madonna and of Christ's childhood.

Botticelli's panel with Mars asleep and Venus waking is, in these terms, not merely—or not only—a graceful, witty mythological scene. Made for a dowry chest, it is an allegory of the conciliation of opposites which makes a happy marriage. Ficino said that the power of Venus makes mock of the violence of Mars—and her pet satyrs in Botticelli's picture do just that. Venus calms Mars's fierce temper and thereby masters him, but mere Force can never, in turn, master Love. Yet the two are not antagonistic. In union, they form a *discordia concors*, the dissonance which is a part of every perfect harmony.

The study of pictorial space and the rethinking of the age-old bases of philosophy were not aims in themselves. Their only end was to define the physical and spiritual world of Man. The definition had, perforce, to begin with the body of man himself, freed of the accident of clothing. For the first life-sized freestanding nude statue since Antiquity, Donatello chose to present the Biblical David as a nude stripling conceived like a Greek statue but with freer movement, with more feeling for man's ability to move and act for himself. This is no subjective impression but a fact born out of masterly use of *contrapposto*: all the body weight rests on one fixed leg while the other hangs free ready to step forward, the shoulder above the weight-bearing leg droops, the other is raised, and bone and musculature twist at the haunches in arrested movement. By 1440 the essence of human anatomy was understood with as much precision as that anatomy of space we call perspective.

The classical poise of Donatello's *David* belies the grim subject. Violence is better expressed in Pollaiuolo's fully clothed *David* with its intense color, menacing slate background, untidy buskins, and the horrible head of Goliath. But it is the nude beneath the clothing which truly gives force to the figure, and that is why Renaissance artists often first did nude drawings and only then clothed them.

Donatello (1386–1466). David. c. 1430. Bronze, height 62$^1/_4$".
National Museum of the Bargello, Florence.

Donatello. Singers' Pulpit (Cantoria). 1433–39. Marble with colored glass inlay ornamentation, 11′5″ × 18′8³/₈″. Museum of the Opera del Duomo, Florence.

Donatello's vision of Antiquity was not limited to the classical equilibrium of his *David*. By the 1430s the Humanists had arrived at a concept of the Greek past in which tragedy and Dionysiac ecstasy also had their place, and what Donatello saw on a second trip to Rome around 1432 struck a responsive chord in his naturally vehement personality (his late reliefs for Padua and for San Lorenzo in Florence are more than Gothic in violence). For his *cantoria* in the cathedral, he took from Roman sarcophaguses the motif of amors dancing and singing, but transformed the cherubs into infant maenads in an unbridled bacchanal set in a Hellenistic exuberance of designs taken over bodily from Antiquity. Startling as this rout of pagan animal spirits may seem in a Christian church, the Renaissance was not shocked: it interpreted it—consistently, in its terms— as the visual symbol of the acclamation *Assumpta est Maria*—"Mary is taken up into Heaven, the angels rejoice and, mingling their praises, bless the Lord, alleluia!" Soon sphinxes and Tritons accompanied the Evangelists' traditional symbols, the angel, lion, bull, and eagle.

From Ghiberti, who began as a goldsmith and worked chiefly in relief, Donatello learned movement and grace, the animated play of fine detail. From Nanni di Banco he learned to convey the solemn grandeur of the sculptural mass. But Nanni died early, and his Four Crowned Saints scarcely clash in style with the Gothic niche into which they are set. They have a noble Roman solemnity, and the middle two heads imitate Roman portrait busts, but they seem fixed to the wall like those Gothic statues which serve also as pillars on church façades. What Nanni achieved, and what no Gothic sculptor could have done, was to give classical form to a classical sentiment of moral grandeur and to create a group statue whose figures are as intimately linked as Masaccio's in the *Tribute Money* done a decade or more later.

The distance between Nanni's art and that of the Renaissance can be measured by another group set in a wall of Orsanmichele. The niche designed by Donatello and Michelozzo where Verrocchio's later Christ and Doubting Thomas enact their drama is Renaissance with a framework of fluted Corinthian pilasters, classical cornice, and half-shell vault supported by Ionic columns. But the figures stand free, are no longer part of architecture, and their emotion is rendered by their motion—and this, above all, was something that could only be conceived out of the Renaissance awareness of man as a free spirit whose inmost feelings are expressed in the action he himself chooses to take.

Nanni di Banco (c. 1390–1421). The Four Crowned Saints. 1410–14. Marble, about life-size. Orsanmichele, Florence.

Andrea del Verrocchio (1435–88). The Incredulity of Saint Thomas. Completed 1483. Bronze, life-size. Orsanmichele, Florence.

By the second half of the century, the austere Roman ideal was giving way, in sculpture, to a native Tuscan sweetness. Forms borrowed from Antiquity were losing their aura of the fabulous past and were taking on a development of their own. Nowhere is this more clear than in funeral monuments. The Gothic tomb had often been set into an elaborately carved niche in a wall, with an effigy of the dead man recumbent on a bier. But here the niche has been opened up into a shallow vaulted chapel (compare Masaccio's *Trinity*). All planes are used from foreground to background, and architecture and sculpture—freestanding and relief—are fused into a plastic unity. The monument rises from a pedestal with a relief of cornucopia-bearing

angels, heraldic unicorns, a garland, and a death's head. On a classical bier lies the effigy of the dead man, attended by two *putti*, the child-angels the Renaissance had fashioned from the pagan Genii. Kneeling angels look down from two elaborate pilasters. Above, in low relief on the wall, a round medallion of the Madonna is borne aloft by two angels, exactly like the portrait of the deceased on a Roman sarcophagus. Finally, the arch is framed by a loose-hanging drapery of marble, a perfect but slightly incredible illusion added to all the others in this monument where marble seems as ductile as wax or velvet. The Gothic tomb was still as death. Here the wind of life ruffles the angels' garments, and even the Cardinal turns on his side as if in sleep.

Antonio Rossellino (1427–79). Funeral Monument of the Cardinal of Portugal. c. 1461–66. Marble, formerly painted and gilded. San Miniato al Monte, Florence.

The wall tomb was not the only form used in the Renaissance. Pollaiuolo turned to another Gothic tradition, the flat grave marker with an effigy of the defunct in low relief set into church floors. This he elevated to the top of a catafalque without, however, sacrificing the impression of a funerary slab: only the Pope's head is in high relief, the body taaers down almost to flatness except for the feet. The bier is covered by a sumptuous fringed brocade (of bronze!) and is surrounded by twelve reliefs of the Seven Virtues, the Della Rovere insignia, and an epitaph. The most extraordinary innovations are reserved for the flanks of the catafalque. In ten irregular compartments, separated by acanthus fronds, are the Seven Liberal Arts plus, as befits a learned pontiff, Theology, Philosophy, and—amazingly—Perspective. At first thought, the latter seems more apt to an artist than to the head of the Church. But Perspective here stands for Science, that other face of the Renaissance in which its adventure was as daring, and as successful, as in art. Perspective was that poetry of science, that science of art, which drove the generations between Uccello and Leonardo almost to madness. So nothing more truly symbolizes the Renaissance than the science which man devised in order to comprehend space, master it, and instill into it the kind of order we call art.

Of scarcely less note is Pollaiuolo's fiendish virtuosity. Here metal curls, twists, falls in pleats, becomes leaf, flesh, hair, brocade. There is a superabundance of details for the sheer joy of doing the impossible. Rossellino's monument, for all its finicky delicacy, has a classical simplicity that never violates Alberti's definition of Beauty. Pollaiuolo's is already too monumental, too rich. This, too, was part of the Renaissance, and it is wrong to think of that art as austerely chaste. But whenever any one element of a style, be it expression or skill, becomes excessive, that style is doomed to die or change. The rise of Rome, with its pomp and ambition, would inevitably lead the artists of Tuscany—Pollaiuolo now, Michelangelo later—to overreach themselves, to speak a more florid language than their native Tuscan idiom.

Antonio del Pollaiuolo. Tomb of Pope Sixtus IV. 1493. Bronze, length 14'7¹/₄". Vatican Grottoes, Rome.

Nothing shows more clearly than the portrait bust how much the Renaissance owed to ancient Rome, how much to itself. The earliest portrait busts, done in the 1450s, were undoubtedly imitations of the Roman busts; but they owed as much to medieval reliquaries portraying the head of the saint they enshrined. Yet Antique and medieval busts were impersonal, more the image of a man's public dignity than of his private foibles. What the Renaissance achieved was a picture of men and women as they are in life, grasping or generous, devious or forthright (compare Mino da Fiesole's *Niccolò Strozzi*, p. 30), single-minded or prone to fashions like this young woman in the Florentine costume stylish in her day. Marble tends to idealize individual traits, so Florentines often preferred the warmer, more fleshlike—and more economical—terra cotta, and every bride had two works of art made for her: a trousseau chest with painted panels to carry to her new home, a portrait bust to leave behind. And with each child she received gifts on a *desco da parto*, a birth salver painted with scenes of the Nativity, often by the greatest of artists.

Domenico Ghirlandaio ▶ (1449–94). Saint Gregory Foretells Death to Saint Fina, from the cycle The Life of Saint Fina. c. 1475. Fresco. Collegiata, San Gimignano.

Desiderio da Settignano (c. 1428–64). Bust of a Young Woman. c. 1455–60. Marble, height 18¹/₈″. National Museum of the Bargello, Florence.

The artist was in no way obliged to dress his personages in Antique garb, not even in Biblical scenes. What was reborn was not, after all, Antiquity but, rather, man's awareness of his own worth. In the North, the Flemish did not hesitate to mingle figures in contemporary costume with others wearing timeless draperies, but there was always something innocent about it, as if belief had to be suspended in face of a miraculous event. The Italian attitude toward religion and life was not disturbed by such contradictions (as early as Masaccio's *Tribute Money*, the tax collector looks as if he had just left his post at one of Florence's city gates). With Ghirlandaio there are, in addition, glimpses of domestic interiors with brass plates, carafes, half-eaten fruit—what later came to be called "genre painting." It is often claimed that such representations of everyday life came into Italy through contact with Flemish art. There is equally good reason to ascribe it to a native tradition of popular art found in devotional images, birth salvers, *cassone* panels (like Uccello's *Hunt*), and, most of all, the *predellas*, those small scenes at the base of large altarpieces where episodes from a saint's life were narrated in easily understandable terms and with a freer technique, contrasting with the majestic image enthroned in the main panel (the Fra Angelico *Martyrdom* is an example). For the first time with such a master of fluid, clear narration as Ghirlandaio, those scenes took their place even in large frescoes where they made miracles seem more credible and stories more vivid.

Everyday activities of peasants and workmen had long been a familiar theme in art. The months of the year and their labors were depicted in small reliefs on the portals of Romanesque and Gothic cathedrals, as well as in the miniatures which brightened the pages of missals and Books of Hours. The tapestries used to cover cold walls were bound soon to adopt the theme. City dwellers saw nothing odd in decorating their palatial homes with tapestried scenes of the folk at work. For all that peasant labors are depicted, nothing in the Renaissance was ever wholly realistic: along with the heraldic escutcheon of the owner there is also the sign of the Zodiac, and something in the scene suggests an ancient ritual performed in a modern world.

At the Palazzo Schifanoia ("Sans-Souci"), the pleasure palace of the Este in Ferrara, the ritual of nature with all its secrets is explained. In a large hall covered completely by frescoes (several—alas!—now ruined), homage is paid to Duke Borso d'Este as the terrestrial ruler whose power and virtues are gifts of the planets which rule all Creation, man and nature alike. The Renaissance inherited its astrological notions from the

◀ Benedetto da Milano (active early 16th century), possibly on designs by Bramantino (1455–1536). The Month of June, from the Trivulzio Months. c. 1503. Tapestry, woven in Vigevano. Castello Sforzesco, Milan.

Francesco del Cossa (c. 1436–78). Pruning Vines, detail of the Month of March in the cycle of Months. c. 1469. Fresco, entire Month 14′9¹/₈″ × 13′1¹/₂″. Palazzo Schifanoia, Ferrara.

Middle Ages, but enriched them with a more authentic knowledge of the planetary gods and a more comfortable familiarity with the things of the earth. On the fresco devoted to the month of March, Minerva, goddess of Wisdom, rides across the top in a fantastic triumphal chariot attended by judges and by chaste maidens weaving. Below this is the Ram, the sign of the Zodiac, in company with two enigmatic figures, one in rags, one richly dressed. In the lowest tier, Borso performs his office of judge and then rides off to the hunt; in the background peasants solemnly—ritualistically, even—prune their vines. The Schifanoia frescoes are an extraordinary transposition of the tiny images of manuscript illuminations to large wall surfaces. For all their strange content and innumerable fine details, these frescoes respect the criterion of the Renaissance: to render the incredible credible by means of superbly controlled composition and plastically rendered volumes, and this lesson was first learned in Ferrara from Piero della Francesca, later from Mantegna.

Cosmè Tura (c. 1430–95). Allegorical Figure. c. 1460–63. Panel, $45^5/_8 \times 28''$. National Gallery, London.

Ferrara, in any case, was somewhat different from Florence. A still-feudal duchy, its tourneys and jousts, courts of love and hunts kept fresh the myth of the "Parfit Knight" that elsewhere had waned with the Middle Ages. And for a knight to be perfect, there must be weird beasts to fight, dragons and basilisks, and so the medieval myths joined the gods of Antiquity awakened from a millennial sleep by the Renaissance. Not that Ferrara was shut off from the outside world: artists came from everywhere—Pisanello from Verona, Jacopo Bellini from Venice, Piero della Francesca from Tuscany, Mantegna from Padua, Rogier van der Weyden from Flanders, Pannonio from distant Hungary, all attracted by the largesse of the Este from which profited also the composers Dufay, Obrecht, and Josquin, and the poet Ariosto. But Ferrara's special half-Gothic and half-Renaissance character is summed up by its finest native painter, Cosmè Tura. This enigmatic figure designed for Borso d'Este's *studiolo* sits like a Madonna or a saint (though she holds a cherry branch, not a palm) on a throne of spiky, gold-hard, jewel-eyed dolphins. She seems to be made of sheets of metal sharp as a razor folded over and over almost to the point of cracking, a creature more mineral than flesh. If she represents Spring, as has been proposed, then it is a notion of springtime as far removed from Botticelli's gentle *Primavera* as the chiseled, cold style Tura derived from Mantegna is remote from the delicate linearity of Florence.

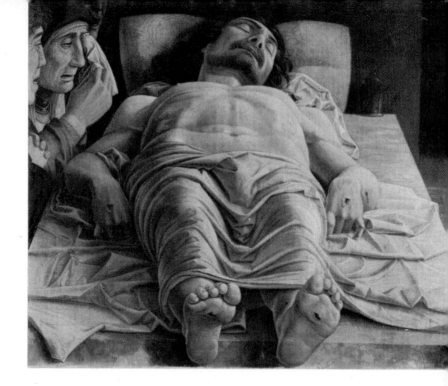

Andrea Mantegna (1431–1506). The Dead Christ. c. 1480. Canvas, $26^3/_4 \times 31^7/_8''$. The Brera Gallery, Milan.

Andrea Mantegna. The Introduction of the Cult of Cybele and the Triumph of Scipio. c. 1500. Canvas, $28^3/_4 \times 105^1/_2''$. National Gallery, London. ▼

Though Venice looked eastward toward Byzantium and its hieratic icons and mosaics, it also had a special relationship with Florence. As early as the 1420s, Florentine artists worked there or in Padua on the mainland. Uccello, Filippo Lippi, Castagno, Donatello, Verrocchio brought the new language with them, and the new art of Flanders also made its way there. Stirred by contact with the noble classical past and the audacious present, the Paduan Mantegna broke decisively with Venetian tradition. The learned humanists at the University of Padua gave him a taste for archaeologically exact reconstruction of the Roman past, Donatello's reliefs in Padua taught him what drama lay in the tense and fine-drawn line, what tragedy in human flesh and muscle, what excitement in the daring rape of space by perspective and foreshortening. Henceforth his art would always oscillate between an almost expressionist foreshortening of the figure in space and a cool, classical painting in relief so low and with a palette so limited as to appear more like stone than like pigment on canvas, board, or wall.

Andrea Mantegna. Scenes from the Court of the
Gonzagas. Completed 1474. Fresco cycle, each
wall 19'8¹/₄" × 26'5³/₄". Camera degli Sposi,
Palazzo Ducale, Mantua.

Bartolomeo Vivarini (1432–99). Saint Mark between Saints John the ▶
Baptist, Jerome, Nicholas of Bari, and Paul. 1474. Triptych with gilded
frame, central panel 65 × 26³/₄", side panels 65 × 22¹/₂" each. Santa
Maria Gloriosa dei Frari, Venice.

But Mantegna's art was not unhuman, as is proved by his work for the highly cultured court of Mantua. For
it, Mantegna created a room unique in its kind, which tells us much of how and when the Renaissance moved
from Humanism to humanity. In Florence, Gozzoli had decorated a small chapel in the Medici Palace with
portraits of its owners disguised as the Magi to make it appear that those newcome banker-rulers had an
ancient noble lineage. Fifteen years later, the Gonzagas could be portrayed in everyday dress and activities,
not idealized or ennobled but merely as handsome and urbane as they surely were. The only touch of something special is in the winged *putti* whose hovering presence lends enchantment to this daily world.

The hieratic style of the Vivarini brothers, so much like Mantegna's, scarcely seems out of keeping with the
florid Gothic frame, though their rich coloring lacks Mantegna's cool restraint and is more truly Venetian.

Landlocked Florence was concerned with line, mass, form. Venice, which stands or sinks according to subtle changes of tone to be read in sea and sky, found its natural expression in color. Florentine light defines forms, Venetian melts them down until mostly color remains. Venetian light is in the colors and the colors are in light, and that unity explains the almost mystical calm of Bellini's pictures. Yet space too remains a fact in Bellini's lovingly detailed portrayal of terra firma, as also in the depth created, astonishingly, by the lectern and the foreshortened raised hand in the *Virgin* by Antonello, a Sicilian acquainted with the art of Spain and Flanders whose brief stay in Venice left an indelible impact. With Bellini, even more than the expression of the figures, tonal atmosphere and spatial vastness convey the mood of the *sacra conversazione*, another of those great innovations of the Renaissance, form and subject at one and the same time, in which the Madonna and Saints stand in meditative, silent communication before the miracle of the Child.

Giovanni Bellini (c. 1425–1516). Madonna and Child with John the Baptist and a Female Saint. c. 1504. Panel, 22⅞ × 29⅞″. Accademia, Venice.

Antonello da Messina (c. 1430–79). Virgin Annunciate. c. 1474. Panel, 17¾ × 13⅝″. National Museum, Palermo. ▶

Giovanni Bellini and Titian (c. 1478/88–1576). The Feast of the Gods. 1514. Canvas, 67 × 74″. National Gallery of Art, Washington, D.C.

Paradoxical as it may be, Venice was also very down-to-earth. The Madonnas of Bellini and Antonello could not be more peasant-humble, and the gods, who elsewhere in Italy appeared divinely nude or sumptuously draped, turned up in Venice looking like strolling players about to perform *A Midsummer Night's Dream*—Mercury with a tureen for helmet, Jove swilling, Priapus dressed like Bottom the Weaver and behaving like a cad. Yet there is magic in the scene, and calm: the feast of the gods is no carousal (compare the Mannerist paintings by Giulio Romano and Wttewael) but a silent dream in an Arcadian landscape which was repainted by Titian to accord with the three pictures he did for the same room in the Este palace at Ferrara, among them the *Homage to Venus* we shall see later.

Vittore Carpaccio (c. 1455–1525). Arrival of Saint Ursula and Her Attendants at Cologne, from the cycle The Story of Saint Ursula. 1490. Canvas, 9′2¹/₄″ × 8′4³/₈″. Accademia, Venice.

The Venetian fascination with people, places, and things was perhaps not alone a matter of the *genius loci* but something learned from their contact with Flemish art which, as it were, held a hand lens up to nature. Bellini's gentle world is vegetable. That of the great narrative cycles his townsman Carpaccio painted for the Venetian *Scuole* is mineral, the hard facts of brick and armor. But it too glows with the amber light of Venice which transforms the Rhine at Cologne into a strangely beautiful Adriatic seaport. Above all, Carpaccio was a *cantastorie*, one of those men still to be found in Italy who sit in public squares and chant great epics in the local dialect. And this too the Renaissance considered a worthy task for painting: to tell a story in vivid, convincing language.

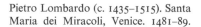

Pietro Lombardo (c. 1435–1515). Santa Maria dei Miracoli, Venice. 1481–89.

Venetian indifference to Tuscan and Roman precepts and models extended to its architecture and sculpture. Only one Renaissance law was obeyed in this church, that of making the façade correspond to the interior structure. Here the entire nave lies under a single vast barrel vault which is terminated abruptly at the façade. But the resultant semi-circular arch is as Byzantine and Venetian as San Marco itself, and the façade is an almost flat sheet of marble without niches or recesses. Its beauty lies in its inlaid stylized Latin and Greek crosses, bands, circles, and squares of porphyry and serpentine. This too reflects the interior, a single nave without side chapels and with flat walls of inlaid marble. The high altar is set above fourteen marble steps so beautiful that Napoleon wished to rip them out and send them to Paris for his coronation.

Pietro Lombardo. Tomb of Doge Pietro Mocenigo. Completed 1481. Santi Giovanni e Paolo, Venice.

As a sculptor, the same Pietro Lombardo (whose name tells his origin) was intensely aware of the use of light to model figures and give depth to niches. This tomb of a warrior-doge, an entire wall in height, employs the classical vocabulary brought to Padua by Donatello, but its heroic figures are almost abstract, simplified to essentials, austere, with none of the elegiac seductiveness of Florentine tomb statues (look back at Rossellino's tomb). Theirs is an intense stillness, hieratic as the Byzantine art which so recently had been all that Venice knew. There is a cold, stoic dignity about them which belongs to a republican Venice where public office called for men of Roman stamp. In time, Venetian tombs grew to cover entire inner walls of churches, and at Santa Maria Zobenigo all of the outer façade was made a funeral monument to the glory of the Barbaro family.

59

This colossal monument is a public homage to the mercenary military leader Colleoni. Forty years earlier, Donatello had made a similar monument in Padua, and the ultimate model for both was the statue of Marcus Aurelius on the Campidoglio in Rome, which the entire Renaissance took as the paragon of the heroic. The Roman statue is as calm and stoic as the philosopher-emperor it depicts; Donatello's *Gattamelata* is an idealized portrait of a captain of men, and it owes its massive repose to the median line which bisects its perfect profile from the horse's mane to its tail. Verrocchio's commander twists nervously on his horse, scornful of the moment's inactivity, horse and man alike tensed for battle. The face of Donatello's bareheaded Gattamelata is tight-lipped but still; the helmeted Colleoni's eyes burn with impatience, his lips sneer in disdain. In a span of only forty years something had changed in the Renaissance: man had found the dark certainty that the paradise regained would once again be lost.

Andrea del Verrocchio. Equestrian Monument of Bartolomeo Colleoni. 1481–88, fused and completed in 1495 by Alessandro Leopardi. Bronze, height c. 13'. Campo Santi Giovanni e Paolo, Venice.

A new element, a new personality were changing the clear daylight of the Quattrocento. Whether, as some argue, this picture was not painted by Verrocchio himself but by his workshop, what counts is that the angel at the far left seems to hail from another world and deserves the look of wonder his coarser companion directs at him, and that the distant view shimmers as no Florentine landscape, let alone Verrocchio's, had before. It seems to come from an artist who found linear perspective antiquated and, instead, thought in newer terms of aerial perspective to create a world not of geometry but of subjective appearance. In Florence, in the 1470s, that could only be Leonardo da Vinci.

Andrea del Verrocchio. The Baptism of Christ. Begun c. 1470. Panel, $69^5/_8 \times 59^1/_2''$. The Uffizi, Florence.

Leonardo da Vinci (1452–1519). The Last Supper. c. 1495–97. Oil-tempera medium on wall, 13′9³/₈″ × 29′10¹/₄″. Refectory, Santa Maria delle Grazie, Milan.

Today we can scarcely "read" the *Last Supper*, so badly has the experimental medium of oil-tempera, used by Leonardo instead of fresco, held up on its damp wall, and so heavily and so often has it been repainted; already in 1556 Vasari found it reduced to a "muddle of blots." Nor, in a less serene time, can we grasp why our grandfathers found this work so worthy of veneration. What awed them was the diversity and beauty of the facial expressions, but those we know were added to the "blots" by restorers and repainters. In an age keenly conscious of abstract form, we instead are moved by its rhythmic composition, musical in its eloquence. Everything converges on Christ, and the central vanishing point is directly behind His head, beneath a classical pediment which frames Him like a halo. Beyond that, the aerial perspective of the dimly perceived landscape acts as a resonating, sympathetic chord. In the foreground, the frieze of disciples undulates like a melody with starts and pauses, gentle conjunct rises and falls, carrying the eye from either margin to the central point—aesthetic and spiritual—of the picture, the Christ. The emotions of each of the disciples can be read in the motions of their bodies and, especially, hands. Emotion through motion was a basic tenet of the Renaissance (medieval gesture was symbolic, and can be read as in a dictionary), and nothing better explains the essentially human aim of all that age's study of anatomy and perspective: communication of a spiritual message depended entirely on the convincing movement of a figure in convincing space.

Leonardo da Vinci. Portrait of a Lady ("Mona Lisa"). c. 1503–5. Panel, 30¼ × 21″. The Louvre, Paris.

As many words have been spent, or wasted, on the *Mona Lisa* as on *Hamlet* without resolving the enigma of either—which in the case of the portrait is certainly not the sitter's name and civil state. The mystery is, rather, how the artist could have conceived the eggshell perfection of the form of the face and of the light which glows from it and not on it— as it does also from the purple satin of the sleeves, and even more from the strange landscape with its suppressed violence (this was the time when Leonardo was obsessed with drawing storms) against which the figure projects so close to the viewer as to make him uncomfortable at the proximity of such beauty. True, we know the names of the technical means Leonardo used: *chiaroscuro*— the play of light against dark; aerial perspective—the paling in color of objects remote from the viewer due to the breaking down of light rays in the aerial space between; *sfumato*—the soft focus, the veil of haze enveloping objects seen at twilight or with eyes half-shut. But these definitions of Leonardo's most extraordinary innovations tell us only what he did, not how he did it, nor, least of all, why. We know how intensely he studied the science of optics, the aesthetics of vision, along with a hundred other fields which had much or little to do with his art. Was it merely the time spent on scientific pursuits which kept him from completing so many admirable projects? Or was it some secret, terrible psychological inhibition, as Freud thought, which makes a mystery beyond explaining—a miracle—of a portrait of a half-smiling woman posed self-consciously before a dimly defined watery landscape which *seems* to have nothing to do with the lady?

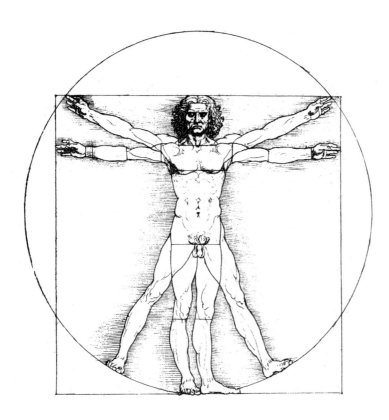

Leonardo da Vinci. Homo ad Circulum (Vitruvian Figure). c. 1485–90. Pen and ink on paper, entire page $13^1/_2 \times 9^5/_8''$. Accademia, Venice.

For the Early Renaissance, the circle was the symbol of God's perfection, but it was also a natural form. For both those reasons, therefore, it was held to be the ideal plan on which to base a place of worship:

Some Temples are round, some square, and others, lastly, have many Sides. It is manifest that Nature delights principally in round Figures, since we find most Things which are generated, made or directed by Nature, are round. Why need I instance in the Stars, Trees, Animals, the Nests of Birds, or the like Parts of the Creation, which she has chosen to make generally round?

LEON BATTISTA ALBERTI,
De re aedificatoria libri X, *1485,*
translated by Giacomo Leoni, 1726.

Just as in Renaissance astronomy the universe circled around Earth, so too the Renaissance ideal was a church centered on man. In Gothic churches, the worshiper is a tiny creature to be led irresistibly to the only focus, the high altar. In the central-plan church of the Renaissance, he is the measure of all things, the center of a perfection which can only be understood fully when man himself views it from the exact center (compare what was said about the Botticelli *tondo*). Whether in never-realized projects by Leonardo, in Raphael's paintings, in churches planned by Brunelleschi, Michelozzo, or Alberti, or built by Giuliano da Sangallo or Bramante, the central plan was, simultaneously, the aesthetic, spiritual, architectonic ideal of the Renaissance.

Raphael (1483–1520). The Betrothal of the Virgin (Lo Sposalizio). 1504. Panel, $66^7/_8 \times 46^1/_8''$. The Brera Gallery, Milan.

The central plan was considered natural, an organic structure in which all parts are congruous and proportionate. This may be why, looking at the round monument Bramante erected on the site of Saint Peter's martyrdom, we experience not awe but pleasure. When it was built, round structures such as the so-called Temple of Minerva Medica (which, in all probability, was really a nymphaeum) still stood on Roman soil, and throughout Italy there were round or octagonal baptisteries from early Christian times. But Bramante grew up in Urbino when Piero della Francesca, with his feeling for perfect harmony of all parts, was still there, and in Milan he frequented Leonardo who filled notebooks with sketches of the ideal church. His Tempietto has been called, with some reason, the first monument of the High Renaissance. As the Early Renaissance belonged chiefly to Florence and Central Italy, so the next phase belonged to Rome, and it is the solemn, grandiose, ambitious, prepossessing character of the City of the Popes that stamps all High Renaissance art. The Tempietto is small, originally about forty feet high, but the rigorous classicism of its components, the purity of its architectonic ornamentation, make it a truly imposing monument—the more so since it is set up on a podium (this effect of "alienation," of monumental elevation, had been used as early as Alberti's temple in Rimini). Moreover, its circular colonnade gives a sculpturesque effect of hollowed-out niches with, in consequence, a play of light and shadow which can be called painterly (some sixty-five years before, Brunelleschi had tried something similar, a wave pattern of projecting apses with half-columns on the exterior of Santo Spirito, but the startled Florentines covered it over as soon as he was dead).

The ground plan of a centralized church need not of necessity be circular. The square, hexagon, and octagon were all tried, but most of all, as in Todi, the Greek cross with four equal arms, each surmounted by a semidome and surrounding an imposing central dome raised high on a drum and crowned by a lantern, a conception which, in essence, was less Antique-Roman than Florentine (compare the cupola of the Duomo of Florence). The domes crowning ancient Roman buildings were massive structures weighing down on the walls. The Renaissance dome seems to grow organically out of the walls and soar lightly upward, its height limited only by the architect's sensitivity to the balance of proportions.

Cola di Matteuccio da Caprarola (active 1494–1518) and others. Santa Maria della Consolazione, Todi. Begun 1504.

Michelangelo Buonarroti (1475–1564). View of the cupola, St. Peter's, Rome. Designed 1558–60. Height of cupola c. 434', diameter 137'9".

Bramante's Tempietto became the basis for his far more grandiose central-plan design for the new St. Peter's—a Greek cross with four apses, so symmetrical that nothing hints at where the high altar was to be placed, and with the main dome surrounded by minor domes and towers over the four corners. Man was no longer the measure in the Rome of the warrior-pope Julius II: the entire length of Brunelleschi's San Lorenzo is less than that of one of the arms of Bramante's Greek cross. Neither brick nor stone would do for such a gigantic structure, only concrete which had not been used since Roman times. But Bramante died, and Michelangelo smashed the classical equilibrium of Bramante's design, condensed the four-armed cross into a single vast open area surmounted by the most colossal cupola any man had ever dreamed of, a dome elongated and not calmly hemispherical, which crashes into the sky with the energy it sucks out of the tense double-columns and compressed windows of the drum and the colossal order of pilasters below, all straining upward to discharge their forces into the ribs that climb the surface of the dome. This is no longer human. It is neither Renaissance, Mannerist, nor Baroque. It is Michelangelo himself, the creator of a terrible sublimity.

Clarity, measure, and restraint belonged to Florence and Central Italy, grandiosity to Rome. In Lombardy, where a still-feudal system and a Northern taste for chivalry and the courtly life did not wholly vanish at a sign from its Humanist philosophers and rulers, the Renaissance manifested itself in exuberance of design and profusion of ornamentation. But superabundance was as much a part of the Renaissance as simplicity and grandeur, and the Renaissance was not confined to Tuscany and Rome. The Certosa of Pavia was built during a span of seventy years by men who, despite the succession of generations, all expressed the native Northern taste for rich decoration. The façade is not a unified conception but a lush compendium of Renaissance forms—a triangular pediment, semicircular arches, niches, medallions, carved cornices, paired columns, statues, reliefs, marble inlays, garlands. By the time it was completed, there had come into being elsewhere— even in Florence and Rome—a new style of architecture in which the wall was "carved" or "molded" to create a surface where light plays a part as important as in relief sculpture and painting. This is the style the French took to be Italian Renaissance (all their military expeditions into Italy passed through Pavia), and when the time was ripe for them to begin their own Renaissance, this became their model, not Tuscan elegance or Roman ponderousness.

Cristoforo Mantegazza (d. 1482), Antonio Mantegazza (d. 1495), Benedetto Briosco (active 1483–1506), Giovanni Antonio Amadeo (1447–1522), Cristoforo Lombardo (active 1510–55), and others. Façade, Certosa of Pavia. 1473–1542.

Luca Signorelli (c. 1450–1523). Madonna and Child. c. 1490. Panel, $66^7/_8 \times 46^1/_4''$. The Uffizi, Florence.

We have seen how architecture changed from repose to tension, how buildings first sat solidly on the ground and later strained upward in defiance of the Renaissance principle of horizontal layers lying quietly one above the other. We have seen, too, how stone surfaces were made to dissolve into a painterly play of light and shade. In painting, much the same occurred. With Signorelli there is already a certain unquiet melancholy in both the Madonna and the Child, so unlike those of Filippo Lippi and Botticelli. And behind them we are startled to find nude Arcadian shepherds, ambiguous in significance in a religious picture, intruders from a pre-Christian age of innocence. Their lean bodies are almost stripped of flesh to expose the tightly drawn

With Perugino, Signorelli's exact contemporary and Umbrian countryman, the hard outlines are softened, smooth flesh veils the musculature, an otherworldly sentimentality makes Apollo and his rustic rival so abstractly disembodied that they scarcely seem to rest solidly on the earth of a fantasy landscape no more real than they are. Sodoma's martyred saint, a High Renaissance work, strains forward and upward, all his musculature and its action clearly defined, not by hard drawing as in Signorelli, but by a sensual, even voluptuous use of paint. The landscape behind him is depicted with the same overt enjoyment of the power of paint to render palpable textures.

Giovanni Antonio Bazzi, called Sodoma (1477–1549). Saint Sebastian. 1525. Canvas, $81^1/_8 \times 41^1/_2''$. Galleria Palatina, Palazzo Pitti, Florence.

Pietro Perugino (c. 1450–1523), attributed. Apollo and Marsyas. Panel, $15^3/_8 \times 11^3/_8''$. The Louvre, Paris.

muscles, and they harmonize with only one thing in the picture, the rocks and architecture of the background. Yet, seated, standing, or lying, they are firmly attached to earth, as in all Early Renaissance art.

Correggio (c. 1489–1534). Jupiter and Io. c. 1532. Canvas, $64\frac{1}{2} \times 27\frac{3}{4}''$. Kunsthistorisches Museum, Vienna.

The virile musculature of Signorelli's nudes—half-drawing, half-sculpture—showed the way to Michelangelo; Perugino was Raphael's teacher; Sodoma exploited the new painterly approach of Leonardo. It was those three masters of the High Renaissance whose own personal genius destroyed the style they created and brought into being something new we call, for better or worse, Mannerism. To them must be added Correggio. With Correggio, sun-drenched light dissolves flesh and world with unparalleled sensuousness. The world itself is no longer rational—Jove's mask materializes out of his cloud-disguise to kiss the nymph Io. The pyramids and squares of Early Renaissance composition give way to soft diagonals and S-curves. Io's body has nothing to do with earth: though seated, she soars into the cloud, and it was this casting-off of the limitations of flesh which made Correggio's cupola frescoes, and not Michelangelo's Sistine Chapel, the models for the great Baroque ceiling decorations of a century later. If there was ever a mortal blow struck against Renaissance reason and order, it was done by Correggio, but with the gentlest of pats.

The final stage in the process, and the onset of something new, comes with Andrea del Sarto. Softly, intangibly molded by light and shade, his saints and Madonna of the Harpies (so called because of the figures on her pedestal) neither stand, strain, nor soar. The saints' poses are impossible to hold, in a moment the Child will fall, the Madonna's breviary also, and she herself will drop from the pedestal on which she stands propped up by two *putti* whose strength no longer avails.

Andrea del Sarto (1486–1531). The Madonna of the Harpies. ▶
1517. Panel, $81\frac{1}{2} \times 70\frac{1}{8}''$. The Uffizi, Florence.

Raphael the Unsurpassable created pictures so rationally designed that not a hair can move, a wavelet subside, without unbalancing the composition. Raphael was himself at last surpassed, not by others but by himself, though it was pupils like Giulio Romano who drove him over the brink. These two frescoes were done at the same time, but Giulio's role was less in the *Galatea*. The *Galatea*, for all its apparent motion, cannot, dare not move. The sea-nymph and her escort are frozen forever in the pyramid within a pyramid of the composition. They are the "frozen music" of the High Renaissance. The *Expulsion of Heliodorus* is something else. Above the still center of the sky with the High Priest in prayer below, the three double arches seem to whirl around, leaving the center of the picture as deserted as the eye of a tornado. The figures are flung out centrifugally, the boys at the upper left appear to be whipped around the columns they are climbing. Giulio's dramatic group at the right—the real subject of the picture—is an unsteady storm of figures; Giovanni da Udine's women at the

◄ Raphael, assisted by Giulio Romano (c. 1492–1546). Galatea. 1511. Fresco, 9'8¹/₈" × 7'4⁵/₈". Villa Farnesina, Rome.

Raphael with Giulio Romano and Giovanni da Udine (1487–1564). The Expulsion of Heliodorus from the Temple. 1511–12. Fresco, width at base 24'7¹/₄". Stanza di Eliodoro, The Vatican, Rome.

left shrink back. Only the static group in the left foreground with Julius II borne aloft is typically Raphael's—uninvolved, posed, composed.

The *Galatea* was painted in the lovely Villa Farnesina of Prince Chigi. It is pure Raphael, a work of utmost if frigid elegance. No matter how much torsion the figures show, there is no strain, not a muscle aches. These are poses, not the stuff of life. However much or little his assistants contributed to it, this is the work of Raphael the consummate artificer. The *Heliodorus* (p. 75) was painted in the Vatican, and a few rooms away Michelangelo was finding forms to express his innate violence, a sculptor carving massive figures in paint on the ceiling of the Sistine Chapel, figures that breathe, move, squeeze the air out of space with their tremendous muscular bulk, painted figures that seem like blocks of marble twisted into strange shapes by their creator's giant hands, figures that—in brief—were *new*. They, like Giulio's Heliodorus sprawled beneath the hoofs of the angelic messenger's steed, took inspiration from the Late-Hellenistic statue of *Laocoön* dug up in Rome in 1506, with its figures writhing in the coils of serpents. But to Raphael and his associates the *Laocoön* suggested only previously untried ingenious poses. Only Michelangelo understood that in it "the body 'acts out' the spirit's agony" (Janson). There is no hint of this in the drunken *Bacchus* he sculpted at twenty-one, still under the spell of the Florentine Academy's Socratic notions in which physical beauty was taken as expressive of the perfect equilibrium of the senses, intellect, and spirit. But his own saturnine temper and his *furor poeticus* (a new notion in the history of the arts) became combined with the Roman obsession that art must strain for a grandeur beyond the limits of man; and Michelangelo turned inward, face

Michelangelo. Bacchus. 1496/97. Marble, height 6'9½".
National Museum of the Bargello, Florence.

to face with his own hopeless striving to achieve the unachievable—"*La mia allegrezza è la maniconia, E'l moi riposo son questi disagi*" (My only joy is melancholy, My only rest these weary trials), he wrote later. It was more than spite that made Raphael, in his *School of Athens*, portray Michelangelo in the guise of the philosopher Heraclitus, that melancholic who despaired of man and found vanity in all things. It was also a grudging tribute to a new kind of artist and, perhaps, even to a new kind of art which, unlike Raphael's, aimed not at beauty of appearances but at expression of man's soul, be it beautiful or ugly, in a state of grace or damned. With such an aim, mere imitation of Antique art was meaningless. Michelangelo created his own "Antiquity," an Old Testament world of huge forms from before the beginning of history, epical creations of divine beauty possessed of more than human force, a vision of man as he was at the Creation, before the daily cares of history had nibbled away at his giant powers. Michelangelo's nudes are not "classical." They are the classical ideal reconceived in terms of a Judaeo-Christian civilization.

The frescoes Raphael and his aides painted in the Vatican *Stanze* take their subjects from the intellectual life and the history of the Church. They are Humanist and aristocratic in their serene equilibrium, their insistence on the ideal forms of beauty. They are also the art of a born courtier, with portraits of Julius II and Leo X as well as of Raphael's friends interspersed among the heroes of action and intellect. They are soft and warm in color, pure in form. Michelangelo's fresco on the vault of the Sistine Chapel—more than 118 by 42 feet in size—is a vast compendium of the earliest history of man before the Covenant, an epic of sin and suffering. The titanic scenes are interlarded not with portraits of contemporaries but with mighty prophets and sibyls and their genii, symbols of divine inspiration, and with seated nude youths who, in an infinite variety of twisting poses, personify the human spirit. Despite the great number of nudes, there is nothing sensuous or sensual in the coloring. It is sculptor's color, sometimes stony as marble, but infinitely gradated to bring out every hint of relief.

Michelangelo. The Great Flood (detail). 1508–9. From a section of the vault frescoes (1508–12), entire section 9'2¹/₄" × 18'8³/₈". Sistine Chapel, The Vatican, Rome.

In 1505 Michelangelo began the impossible project destined to embitter his life for a half-century, the colossal tomb of Julius II. Both practically and spiritually the grandiose design was beyond the powers of the artist to complete, of his patrons to see through to the end. The monument now in San Pietro in Vincoli, Rome, is unfinished, the great statue of Moses with its sublime *terribilità* dwarfing its oversimplified, reconstructed setting. To France in 1550 were taken two "Slaves" intended for the tomb, one rebellious, one suffering as in death. These are the two poles of the mature Michelangelo's grasp of both life and art: frustrated revolt and the exhaustion of body and spirit which follows. Anatomy here becomes the instrument to express the deepest pathos. Cover over the head with its character of desperate sleep; the body still speaks of the same woe—the torso twisted with fatigue, the right hand too heavy to push back the fetters, all the giant weight bearing down on the right hip and leg.

But Michelangelo saw no release in death, for Judgment waited at the end. In the tombs he made for the Medici, there is no struggle, no effort even, only a vast oppressive resignation before the impossibility of life. As with the tomb of Julius, what we have now is not the artist's original design, which was much more complex. The chapel is a high, square room in which the walls seem to tilt forward menacingly. The tall niches with their tight-spun segmental pediments are crushingly narrow. Huge as is each sarcophagus, it seems too shallow for the corpse within, and the allegorical figures—*Night* and *Day* on one tomb, *Twilight* and *Dawn* on the other—have a weight not to be measured in tons but only on the immeasurable scale of grief. The male body of *Day* is a "majestic landscape of hill and hollow, each undulation tense and purposeful" (Clark), but his strength is of no avail and he stares helplessly from a blind mask. *Night*, racked with dire dreams and fatigue, has the sagged breasts and belly of a woman whose time is done.

Michelangelo. Night, from the Tomb of Giuliano de' Medici. 1526–31. Marble, length 72³/₈″.

The young Giovanni Strozzi, wishing to compliment the master, wrote this conventional epigram: "Night, whom you see here in sweet sleep, was by an Angel carved; this stone but sleeps and, so, hath life: wake her, believe me, and she will speak." Bitter with years, grieving for the death of the Florentine Republic, Michelangelo retorted: "Dear to me is sleep, but even more that I remain of stone while the shame and infamy of men endure; not to see, not to feel, these do I praise: whence, wake me not, pass by, speak low."

"Messer Giorgio, my good friend [wrote Michelangelo to Vasari in a letter dated September 28, 1555], With regard to that staircase for the library, about which so many people are bothering me, believe me that if I could recall just how I planned it, no one would have to ask twice. There comes back to my mind, as in a dream, a staircase, but I scarcely think it that one, so clumsily odd does it seem to me now. But here is what it was to be.... What I describe seems to me now laughable, but I know you will be able to make something of it." What Giorgio Vasari and his colleagues executed for the eighty-year-old master was indeed something that could come only in a dream, a dream of Michelangelo's. There is something touching in the fact that Michelangelo's most personal achievement in architecture should be not St. Peter's but the narrow vestibule of a library housing the manuscripts of the Ancients and Humanists, not in Rome where the old man ended but in Florence where the young man began, and that it should be in the cloisters of the same church, San Lorenzo, where Brunelleschi created the architectural style of the Renaissance, where the young Michelangelo's first patron, Lorenzo de' Medici, was buried with his family, where thirty-five years earlier the mature Michelangelo had begun the great Medici tombs. If his architecture for the funerary chapel seems strange, the library vestibule has that superb wrongness which, in the hands of a great master, is superbly right. The room is excessively high. It is divided horizontally in proportions no rule of architecture authorizes. Every element of structure or decoration contradicts its functional purpose with absurd but breath-

taking illogicality. The pediment above the door breaks without reason, the frames around doors and niches squeeze inward, and their pilasters taper *downward*, not upward, compressing unbearably the already too-narrow niches. Worse, the double-columns support nothing and themselves need support because they are set *into* the wall instead of standing in front of it as they should. Ultimate absurdity, double wall brackets beneath the columns sustain nothing but only hang down uselessly. The staircase itself does not flow upward but seems to ooze downward like a mass of lava. All logic is defied, all movement paralyzed. And yet, this slate-gray, dead-white vestibule has the beauty of Michelangelo's own sonnets—wrong-headed, irregular, overly complex, but profoundly expressive of a great personality. Even architecture here becomes a personal expression, and that is one of the things we mean by Mannerist art.

Michelangelo. Vestibule of the Laurentian Library, Florence. Begun 1524; staircase designed and built after 1555.

Michelangelo. The Last Judgment. 1536–41. Fresco, 44′11″ × 40′. Sistine Chapel, The Vatican, Rome.

Michelangelo. The Rondanini Pietà. 1552–64. Marble, height 6′5¹/₂″. Castello Sforzesco, Milan.

Such an apocalyptic art could only end in the *Last Judgment*, a tremendous composition where, on the left, Titans swirl up to the seat of the vengeful Christ, on the right Cyclopes plunge to Hell. A merciless work—even the Virgin shrinks from the dead in revulsion nobly tinged with pity. The least merciful of all is the artist to himself: at Christ's feet Saint Bartholomew holds his flayed skin on which Michelangelo has painted a desperate, grimacing self-portrait. The times had changed from the heroic days of the Sistine ceiling frescoes. Revolt had sprung up inside and outside the Church, and a thoughtless world had awakened to the cataclysm its greatest artist had prophesied in poems, pictures, and statues. But Michelangelo grew old, and in his soul the ashes of misery replaced the fires of rebellion. He returned to sculpture, his one—he said his only—love. His final three statues are all *Pietàs*, the last of them this strange creation at which he still worked on the eve of his death. It is unfinished—*nonfinito*. Not only is there none of the high polish which is the sculptor's patient equivalent for the painter's sensuous, light-enhancing glazes, but the forms themselves scarcely emerge from the block. The dead Christ is forever part of the body of the Mother, an arm remains from an earlier version, the faces are abstract masks. Yet, the forms which do emerge are so completely new, so far beyond the thought of any sculptor, that perhaps Michelangelo knew in advance that such a terrifyingly personal, profoundly felt conception could never be completed by mortal hand and brain. The notion of the *nonfinito*, the work left in the rough, was exploited by his Mannerist followers as no more than a device to give an effect of spontaneity, just as they transformed his high spiritual conception of the nude into a play of sensuous, sensual forms of flesh. But the aspiration was not lost, nor the dramatic sense of man's tragedy, and this too was part of the new style, Mannerism, which was Michelangelo's heritage.

This council hall in a fortress was arranged under Paul III as a refuge for the papal court in the event of another such disaster as the sack of Rome in 1527 by the imperial lansquenets. The lavish decoration is due to Perin del Vaga of Florence, who had also worked in Pisa and Genoa, to Pellegrino Tibaldi of Bologna, Ancona, Turin, Milan, and, later, Madrid, and to Marco Pino of Siena and finally of Naples; their helpers came from all over Italy. This Italian "internationalism" ushered in the new style, Mannerism, which quickly became the only style in every corner of Europe, a truly international language though one with many personal accents and local dialects. An art born of the elegant grace of Raphael, the luminous sensuality of Correggio, the naked violence of Michelangelo, many of its traits are already obvious here. Allegory and history intermingle, and each scene has multiple meaning. The nude, draped or not, is everywhere, but the individual figure is drained of significance to become merely a decorative motif. The separate arts are united and confused: stucco sculpture looks soft as painting, monochromatic painted panels imitate carved bas-reliefs, the walls seem to be sheathed in marble, gold, and bronze but are only painted; the ultimate illusion—*trompe l'oeil*—is applied in painted half-open doors through which painted servants scurry in and out in an astonishingly realistic manner (perhaps to help besieged prelates to feel less claustrophobic in this high citadel). Senses and materials swim in confusion, illusionistic painting becomes a conjuror's trick, and above all there is a *horror vacui*—every free space is filled in

Perin del Vaga (1501–47), Pellegrino Tibaldi (1527–96), and Marco Pino (c. 1525–c. 1588). Sala Paolina, Castel Sant'Angelo, Rome. Decoration begun around 1545.

with gilded, painted, stuccoed cupids, vases, medallions, garlands, and all of them are no more "real" than tinsel.

Whatever the subject might be, the nude was *de rigueur*. Michelangelo had proved this by covering the Sistine Chapel with a plethora of naked bodies, though not without arousing protest—the Dutch pope Adrian VI called it a "vulgar bathhouse," Pius IV commanded Daniele da Volterra to paint draperies over the genitals in the *Last Judgment*. But the new Mannerist nude was svelte, languid, sophisticated, sensual, never heroic or a symbol of spirituality—a highly aristocratic form which, in the no longer republican Florence of Duke Cosimo I, was so much the more needed because the new Medici rulers had mere bankers as ancestors.

Benvenuto Cellini (1500–71). Perseus with the Head of Medusa. 1553. Bronze, height 17'3/4" with marble and bronze pedestal. Loggia dei Lanzi, Florence.

Benvenuto Cellini. Danaë with the Child Perseus, on the pedestal of the Perseus statue. Marble pedestal, height 6'6³/4"; bronze figure group, height 37³/4".

Benvenuto Cellini. The Salt-cellar of François I. 1539–43. Gold and enamel on ebony base, $10^1/_4 \times 13^1/_8''$. Kunsthistorisches Museum, Vienna.

The ideal nude was no longer a plowboy or peasant girl undressed, but the very image of the refined beauty which aristocracy attributed to itself. Cellini's Perseus is a lithe young man and fine-muscled—virtuosity in depicting muscular anatomy became, in this period, what skillful play with perspective had been earlier. The pedestal on which he stands swarms with motifs borrowed from Antiquity, but they have more to do with decoration than with any return to a classical past. The Danaë on the pedestal takes her pose from Michelangelo's *Dying Slave*, but the body relaxes in languorous grace, not tragic exhaustion. The deep-lying spiritual symbolism of the Renaissance gives way to an ingenious play of allegorical conceits: on the saltcellar Cellini made for King François I, Neptune, god of the sea, and Ceres, goddess of earth, symbolize their union in producing salt; around the base are small reliefs representing the Four Seasons and the Four Times of Day, but now it is a table ornament that bears the cosmic symbols Michelangelo had introduced into his tombs for the Humanist-minded earlier Medici. In the next generation, with Ammannati and Giambologna (Jean Boulogne of Douai in French Flanders, who settled in Italy at the age of sixteen), the nude became even more slender, with elongated legs and a torso tapering up through an exaggeratedly long neck to a tiny head—the flickering flame on a candle bent into the shape of an S. The nude, alone or as a group, coiled on itself to form a *figura serpentinata*—a convolvulus vine, a burst of flame, a jet of water, or a Roman candle (the age was mad for fountains and fireworks), anything except hard, resistant, intractable bronze or marble. Mere matter must no longer be an impediment to the artist's fantasy.

Bernardo Buontalenti (1536–1608). Oval vase. 1583. Lapis lazuli, height 16″, width 4³/₄″; mounting in enameled gold by Jacopo Bilivert (1550–93). Museo degli Argenti, Palazzo Pitti, Florence.

Giambologna (1529–1608). The Rape of the Sabines. 1583. Marble, height c. 13′6″. Loggia dei Lanzi, Florence.

Whether giant statue, tiny statuette, fountain, or vase, the emphasis was always on elegance of silhouette, polished grace, and, ultimately, on the most daring feats of craftsmanship worthy of admiration in and for themselves.

The most daring was Giambologna's. Renaissance statues, even Michelangelo's, were designed to be viewed from one position primarily, though the other sides might not lack in fascination. Here, though, is a statue with three quite different figures locked in a single upward spiral, the first large-scale work to present a startling, aesthetically satisfying view from every angle.

Andrea Calamech (1529–89). Water Nymph on the Neptune Fountain by Bartolomeo Ammannati (1511–92). 1560–75. Bronze and marble, figure over life-size. Piazza della Signoria, Florence.

Refinement of taste leads to a delight in the untoward and even bizarre (think of the *Art Nouveau* of the 1890s). In the early Cinquecento, "*Roma sotterranea*" was opened up—the long-buried grottoes and the Golden House of Nero. Their decorative motifs of fantastic sphinxes, monsters, trophies, arabesques, candelabra were seized upon as an exciting addition to the repertory of classical forms. *Grotteschi* appeared everywhere: on ceilings and walls, frames (even the surrounds of Raphael's Biblical scenes in the Vatican loggias), carved furniture, majolica plates, and tableware such as this water cooler made by the Fontana family who, in the works they executed for the great courts, were responsible along with Raphael and his followers for spreading the vogue for *grotteschi* throughout Europe.

Profiting from Michelangelo's demonstration of architecture as personal expression, Mannerist buildings were no less imaginative. The Palazzo Farnese is still very High Renaissance in its compact, Roman monumentality, though its inner court, not shown here, already has some of the repressed tension associated with Mannerism. But the willful illogicality of Mannerism makes of the Palazzo Massimo a fascinating but anti-architectural work of architecture. The deep-set entrance loggia shrouded by columns creates a variegated play of light and darkest shadow which has more to do with Leonardo da Vinci's painting than with Alberti's architectural logic. The windows of the first story are too shallow, those of the upper stories too small and, moreover, are set in frames as delicate as paper cutouts. And the entire façade curves, as if the curving street in front had gently but insistently forced it back at the sides in a way impossible—seemingly—to any structure made of brick and stone.

Antonio da Sangallo the Younger (c. 1485–1546). Palazzo Farnese, Rome. Begun 1514, redesigned 1534, upper story added by Michelangelo after 1546.

◄ Workshop of the Fontana Family. Water cooler from the table service of the Duke of Urbino. c. 1560. Majolica, 13 × 18^1/$_2$″. National Museum of the Bargello, Florence.

Baldassare Peruzzi (1481–1536). Palazzo Massimo alle Colonne, Rome. Begun 1532.

In the Quattrocento, the Medici villas around Florence were country dwellings of rather modest dimensions in undisturbed natural settings. A century later, in Rome, the Villa Giulia of Pope Julius III is a superbly stage-managed piece of scenography in which everything conspires to make a reposeful, intimate retreat for a great lord. Its architecture comprises a series of set pieces, like the stage designs Serlio published in 1551 in which straight streets lead through an arch to a distant prospect, or like that constructed for the Teatro Olimpico in 1585. Each section of the building, facing one of the two semicircular courts, is topped by an open loggia, through which the eye is led to the neatly ordered walled garden in the rear. The loggia takes the form of an Antique Roman triumphal arch and surmounts a portico below which is a graceful, concave nymphaeum with an elegant curving balustrade supported by Greek caryatids.

The result, in the Villa Giulia, is a façade in which distant views, a flat but highly varied façade with arches, niches, columns, pilasters, and statues, all interlock with courts and gardens to form a whole, inviting the eye to explore the fascinating variety of details within a carefully controlled unity. Within the same theatrical context, the word "spectacular" is not inappropriate for the garden façade of the Villa Medici. It is a kind of showcase for the Antique Roman reliefs set into its walls, framed by engaged pilasters, bordered by friezes and garlands, the entire wall hollowed out into niches and windows and crowned by two towerlike open loggias. Yet the wall is

Annibale Lippi (latter half of 16th ▶ century). Garden façade of the Villa Medici, Rome. Added around 1580 to the already existing building.

Giorgio Vasari (1511–74), Jacopo Vignola (1507–73), and Bartolomeo Ammannati. Façade of garden pavilion, Villa Giulia, Rome. 1551–55.

singularly flat and, somehow, gives an impression of impermanence, like any stage setting no matter how perfect the illusion, or like one of those great triumphal arches built of flimsy board and stucco and decorated by the greatest of artists for the ceremonial entries of emperors and visiting potentates into conquered or friendly cities. The impression is not unfounded: the pilasters, columns, frames, and all the rest have no true or necessary architectonic function; they are no more than added decoration on a plane surface like that of a picture—or of a stage-set.

The most extraordinary pleasure palace of all was built for Federico Gonzaga as a place to enjoy his public and private loves. Brought to Mantua from Rome by Baldassare Castiglione after the death of Raphael, Giulio Romano erected there a palace which, from the outside, seems too immense and, also, too squat. As a solid block its sheer size would be preposterous. But mostly it is no more than a single room wide and is built around courts and gardens. To avoid monotony, and to create the delectable variety expected in a pleasure palace, Giulio devised a remarkable diversity of façades to face the inner enclosures. What is more, each of them deliberately violates the rules of architecture in a manner surprising to us but surely intended to amuse connoisseurs of the time. All the elements in the one illustrated above are from the classical vocabulary of architecture. But they are isolated, made to stand out both by ingenious framing and by abrupt contrast

Giulio Romano. Palazzo del Tè, Mantua, seen from the garden. 1524/25–34.

with the rough-textured, rusticated flat wall. On the frieze, an occasional triglyph—a small projecting block with vertical grooves—simply slips down out of line, as if the construction were not very secure in the first place. The keystone of the semicircular-arched portal breaks through the triangular pediment above it, and looks like nothing so much as a giant's club brandished over the entrance. Every line is somewhere broken, as if the architect could not resist the fun of moving the pieces on his chessboard into impossible positions. And most of it is false—stone, brick, or stucco pieces stuck onto a flat wall, decoration not construction, a sophisticated stage-set for a sophisticated erotic comedy.

   Inside, Giulio aimed to outdo Raphael and Michelangelo. Marquetry doors opened on to rooms frescoed from top to bottom with themes calculated to flatter and encourage the Duke in his amorous and military pursuits. The rooms to the north, including the Hall of Psyche, are a hymn to erotic pleasure. Those to the south celebrate virile force and victory with the *Fall of the Giants*, a massive, grotesque jangle of broken pillars, rocks, and giants tumbling crazily down a fresco into the crater of Etna (the fireplace below!). *Fare piacere, fare stupore*—titillate, astound—this was the dual aim of Mannerist artists in every field, and even the astounding was meant to titillate refined tastes, except when applied by a few great artists to religious art or in some almost terrifying, half-mad portrait. Mannerist art is not "decadent" (an old, outworn, uncomprehending accusation leveled against it by the nineteenth century which preferred the moral and the pretty), but it catered to decadent tastes. The Psyche frescoes are openly lascivious, with no details spared. In the Early Renaissance, mythology still carried with it an aura of wonder, of primeval awe, and was used more often for its metaphysical or ethical symbolism than for itself. Now, with Mannerism, the old stories were too-often told, their meaning had faded. The gods stood naked in their foibles—the Duke caught with the chambermaid, the Duchess with her page—and artists like Giulio Romano were better at illustrating their vices than their virtues.

If Florence did not lag behind Mantua in games of love, it had other, more intellectual pastimes. The great palace of the Uffizi was built by Vasari not only to house the grand dukes' art collections but also to gather under one roof the workshops where craftsmen and artists turned out everything required for an elegant existence—statues, pictures, fine cloths and tapestries, carved gems, vases in semiprecious stones, table service in gold or silver, perfumes, rare ointments, and medicines (some said poisons). In the Palazzo Vecchio, Vasari designed a secret *studiolo* for the young Francesco I. A strange study room, windowless, airless, lit only by candles, a grotto of night where the melancholy prince could pore over his treasures—chunks of quartz, branches of coral, strange metals from foreign parts, vials foaming with elixirs of life or wealth, deformed animals in which the rules of nature had gone wrong—again, *fare piacere, fare stupore*. The vault and walls are covered with works by Florentine and transplanted Flemish artists (it was in Florence that

Giulio Romano and assistants. The Banquet of Psyche and Eros (detail). Fresco. Hall of Psyche, Palazzo del Tè, Mantua.

The Studiolo of Francesco I de' Medici, Palazzo Vecchio, Florence. Designed by Giorgio Vasari, 1570–72. Visible here: vault fresco, The Four Elements, by Francesco Poppi (1544–97); paintings and bronze statues on upper tier, left wall, Santi di Tito (1536–1603), The Sisters of Phaëton Metamorphosed into Poplars, Mirabello Cavalori (c. 1510/20–72), The Makers of Wool, Alessandro Allori (1535–1607), Coral Fishers, Bartolomeo Ammannati, Venus; upper tier, end wall, Giovanni dell' Opera (1540–99), Juno, Maso da San Friano (c. 1532–71), Diamond Mines, Elias de Witte called Elia Candido (16th century), Zephyrus; lower tier, end wall, Giovanni Maria Butteri (c. 1540–1606), Aeneas Landing in Italy, Maso da San Friano, The Fall of Icarus; lunette above end wall, Agnolo Bronzino (1503–72), Portrait of Eleanora of Toledo.

Giambologna. The Apennine. Completed c. 1580. Natural rock, masonry, and *pietra serena*, height 33′. Villa Pratolino (now Villa Demidoff), near Florence.

Northern realism, which the Italians thought "bizarre," found its most eager response). Every work of art symbolized some recondite myth or allegory pertaining to the Four Elements, and behind each picture was a secret cupboard to store the substance appropriate to the picture's subject. The only "human" note in the room: at one end Eleonora of Toledo looks down with Spanish disdain at her son's fruitless pursuits; at the other, Cosimo I frowns with Florentine dismay at his heir's neglect of the State for study.

But in the strange new world that science and exploration were opening up, Francesco and his city were haunted by Job's question: "But where shall wisdom be found? and where is the place of understanding?" The more the serene rationalism of the Renaissance Humanists faded from mind, the more the answer seemed to be: in Unreason, in the wild, the primitive, the twisted giants and dwarfs of nature—the earth's nature and man's—gone mad. So, in the parks of their new villas, the Medici built weird grottoes of rough stone, and in hidden copses set up giant statues, not of marble or bronze but seemingly hewn out of huge, shell-incrusted rocks, so one could no longer say where nature left off and art began. More fantastic: in this giant's head there is a tiny room where lights were lit to shine out of the monster's eyes. Immensely diverting it all was, and the court was sophisticated enough to enjoy it, but underneath there ran a dark current that the earlier Medici and their artists could never have anticipated.

Raphael. Portrait of Baldassare Castiglione. 1515–16. Panel transferred to canvas, $32^1/_4 \times 26^3/_8''$. The Louvre, Paris.

Jacopo Pontormo (1494–1556). Portrait of a Lady. ► Panel, $35 \times 27^1/_2''$. Städelsches Kunstinstitut, Frankfurt.

Raphael's portrait belongs to the High Renaissance. Its color is warm, friendly even, its character as urbane, reposeful, sympathetic as the writings of Castiglione himself. There is loving attention to details of texture—velvet, soft linen, fur, flesh, and beard. The paint is applied richly, in a "painterly" manner. Pontormo's portrait belongs to Mannerism. Not painterly, it seems to be cast in some enameled metal, and everything has the same hard sheen—hair, flesh, satin and velvet, jewels, books, and furniture. For all its brilliance, the color is cold as the young woman's flesh, cold as her unflinching gaze. Raphael's is the portrait of a courtier by a courtier, both of them aristocratic to the hilt. Pontormo's is a court portrait, but made by a stubborn, solitary man who, we know from himself and his friends, was sick of life. His portraits are not unfeeling, like Bronzino's almost abstract likeness of Ammannati's poetess wife Laura Battiferri. Instead, they mirror inexorably that almost mad resolution to stand up to any horror which made the Medici court of the sixteenth century and its notorious crimes of passion a frequent source of plots for the Jacobean tragedies of lust and blood. Scholars dispute the meaning of Mannerism as term and concept. Some apply it only to Vasari's bella maniera—an elegant, stylish, playful art, more decoration than expression; others find in it only the fantastic, unnatural, and grotesque; still others see it as a many-sided, complex reaction of shock to such events of spiritual significance as the sack of Rome in 1527, the fall of the Florentine Republic in 1530, and the Counter Reformation and, hence, an art which sought to express a new psychological insight. Unless we wish to do violence to fact, we must concede it to be all of these—grottoes and noble palaces, wild flights of fancy and studied elegance, a new and more anguished piety and outright lasciviousness, a daring pre-Freudian descent into the darker regions of the psyche and a cynical satisfaction with surface appearances.

Agnolo Bronzino. Portrait of Laura Battiferri. 1560? Panel, 32⅝ × 23⅝". Loeser Collection, Palazzo Vecchio, Florence.

Northern Italian Crafts- ► man. Necklace. c. 1570. Enameled gold with pearls, rubies, sapphires, and emeralds, length 20½". National Gallery of Art, Washington, D.C.

The fantastic and the decorative trends met in the art of jewelry, as in this necklace, certainly not one of the most extravagant to have survived. In an age which took pleasure in the arcane, even the enameled ruby-set sphinx of the pendant was not without ulterior significance. It derives, beyond doubt, from the craze for *grotteschi* which spread from Rome all over Europe, but also from the allegorical jeweled figures that Cellini devised, and its wearer would have thought of that meaning also. This style of jewelry was probably an invention of northern Italy, and the strapwork pattern of its settings came from Flanders, but by the 1570s goldsmiths everywhere were outdoing each other in inventing weird ornaments in this international style.

There was, from the outset, open conflict between, on the one hand, *grazia, facilità,* and *maniera*—virtues Raphael typified and Vasari propagandized—and, on the other hand, the *terribilità* of Michelangelo. In very oversimplified terms, this was a conflict between "proclassical" and "anticlassical" orientations, between stylish decorativeness and what, today, we call expressionism. Basically it had nothing to do with schools or generations or places where artists worked: Bronzino was Pontormo's pupil from childhood on and his lifelong friend, but in essence (though nothing in his work hints at imitation of Raphael) he belongs in the first category, Pontormo in the second. There were other influences—Correggio's, Leonardo's—but the crux of it was the dialectical struggle between the great lodestars Raphael and Michelangelo. Though that struggle did create differences between school and school, generation and generation, more important were the tensions it induced in individual artists, racking their minds and spirits as if some personal loyalty were at stake. The nightmarish, expressionist paintings of Rosso Fiorentino owed everything to the spirit and nothing—almost nothing—to the letter, of Michelangelo's, and he could only flee to France to become at best a decorator. Bronzino's nudes are epicene reworkings of Michelangelo's, but in this complex allegory of Time and Truth unveiling the evil of Lust, the fine-edged drawing and jewel-like painting have a cerebral sensuality Michelangelo would have dismissed as inexpressive and a decorative treatment he would have thought immoral. For Pontormo there was only one god, Michelangelo, and yet his own misanthropic character, so much like his idol's, could never love outright but must find strange ways of emulation, of rivalry even. Another factor added to his turmoil: around 1515 woodcuts and engravings by Lucas van Leyden and Dürer became known in Florence, and on Pontormo they had a decisive— Vasari said disastrous—impact. The oddness of their forms—partly an inheritance from the Gothic, partly an awkward coming to terms with the Renaissance—was as irresistible to Pontormo as the unorthodox spirituality of their expression. But both form and expression were alien to what Michelangelo stood for, and brought about new, though highly

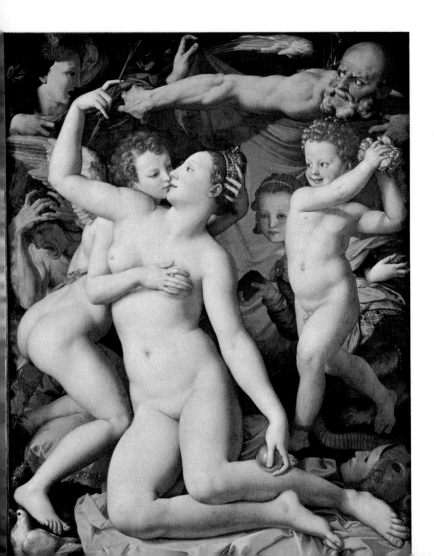

Agnolo Bronzino. Allegory. c. 1546. Panel, 61 × 56³/₄". National Gallery, London.

Jacopo Pontormo. Deposition. 1525–28.
Panel, 10'3¼" × 6'3⅝". Santa Felicita,
Florence.

creative, tensions in Pontormo. In
the *Deposition* his forms coil in an
oval with a rhythm which is unbearably slow, almost viscid, more like
that of Michelangelo's library stairs
than the swooping release of his *Last
Judgment*. Where are these people?
Nothing tells us. There is sky and
ground, but we do not know where
or how the figures stand—or do they
float? This "antispace" itself accounts for much of the supernatural,
mystical oddity of the picture. Do the
personages suffer? grieve? Their
blank stares are those of shock vic-
tims. Their faces are drained of
feeling, their bodies of strength. They droop, wilt, like the withering plants and dried autumn flowers their
acid, yellowed, sick colors remind us of. Space, movement, forms, color—none of these belong to the world
we see but only to the world we feel. The sentiment is not Christian, not universal, but terribly, painfully
personal, and it is fitting that the hypochondriacal thirty-four-year-old Pontormo may have portrayed himself
in the old man who looks out pitiably—not pitifully—from the upper right.

Parmigianino, like Correggio, worked in Parma, and there is much of Correggio's precious luminosity about him, as there is also of Raphael's *grazia*. To him we owe a new canon of beauty, the excessively elongated body tapering up to a small, exquisitely oval head, a type which would spread to Fontainebleau and, thence, throughout Europe. The wave pattern of this body type flows through every element of Parmigianino's pictures, a soft undulation of flesh, drapery, cloud, and sky. Space becomes mysterious and illogical in this universal flow. Usually there is an overlarge figure so close to the viewer as to seem to project from the surface, then suddenly space dwindles to an artifact, as in this *Madonna*, and we puzzle over where the column is, and what it is, and how tall is the tiny prophet alongside. By such means, a picture becomes a poetical myth, a perfumed mystery of supernatural elegance. Other artists had portrayed themselves as in a mirror, but no one had made the optical distortions themselves the subject of a picture, nor performed the trick of painting it on a convex panel.

Parmigianino. The Madonna with the Long Neck. 1534–40. Panel, 7′1″ × 4′4″. The Uffizi, Florence.

◄ Parmigianino (1503–40). Self-Portrait in a Convex Mirror. c. 1523–24. Convex panel, diameter 9⅝″. Kunsthistorisches Museum, Vienna.

Rosso Fiorentino (1495–1540). Moses Defending the Daughters of Jethro. 1521. Canvas, 63 × 46⅛″. The Uffizi, Florence.

Rosso belongs to that other world where the spiritual turmoil of a Michelangelo or Pontormo kneads flesh into stranger, more compelling forms, where reality is not delicately manipulated but outraged. With colors like searing acids impregnating strangely shaped blocks of ice, he dislocates our sense of what is real into a new vision, both emotional and artistic—note the weirdly superimposed silhouettes of the two faces in the upper right corner.

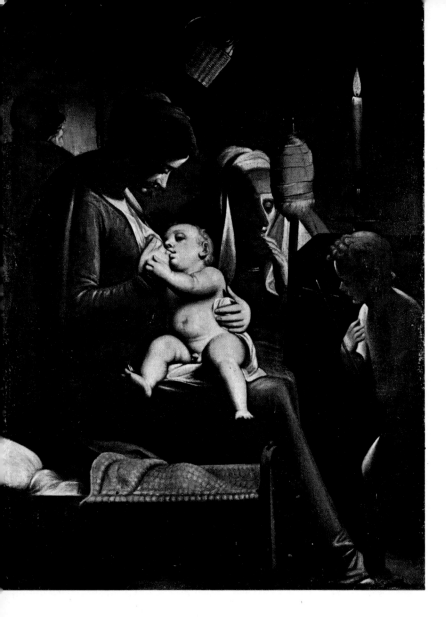

Luca Cambiaso (1527–85). Holy Family. Canvas, $57^1/_8 \times 42^7/_8$″. Palazzo Bianco, Genoa.

Taddeo Zuccari (1529–66). The Conversion ▶ of Saint Paul. c. 1555. Canvas, $26^3/_4 \times 18^1/_2$″. Palazzo Doria-Pamphili, Rome.

This is a startling image to follow those just seen, a plunge from fantasy to realism. A few painters had attempted night scenes before this— Geertgen tot Sint Jans in Haarlem at the end of the fifteenth century, Correggio in Parma—but never with the same regard for humble fact as the Genoese Cambiaso. More striking even are the firm, almost geometric forms of a purity unseen since Piero della Francesca (Cambiaso left drawings in which the human figure is reduced to pure cubistic shapes). Such extreme simplification of forms and atmosphere were to be taken up eagerly in the Baroque by Caravaggio and Georges de La Tour, a convincing proof (much needed!) that the Baroque was an art of order after the subjective disaggregation of forms under Mannerism. But this is *arte sacra*, the expression of the Counter Reformation and of Loyola's *Spiritual Exercises* in which the novitiate was to meditate on images of such realism, such immediacy, that he could, as it were, himself participate in the sacred event. Such images could be of two types: of humble folklike piety such as this, calculated to arouse the tenderest of devotional sentiments, or apocalyptic like Zuccari's *Conversion of Saint Paul* (which owes much to Michelangelo's fresco on the same subject in the Vatican), where the viewer plunges into an awesome sacred event at the highest point of the action. But let there be no mistake: there is as much—or more—artifice, as much *maniera*, in Cambiaso's ingenious rejection of all unessential details as in Zuccari's overloaded, somewhat pretentious, very Roman canvas—which, surprisingly, is less than half the size of Cambiaso's. Just as the dynamism of Mannerism came from the clash between Raphael and Michelangelo, so in the Baroque the driving force was to be the tension between the two currents seen here.

Venice went her own way through the long lives of Giovanni Bellini and Titian who, together, spanned almost a century and a half. Even the brief lesson of Giorgione it could take to itself and profit from—Giorgione whose landscapes, peopled with a few enigmatic figures, give the impression, as do Michelangelo's statues and Leonardo's portraits, that what is depicted, the image itself as we see it, is somehow endowed with "intelligence," an innate power to think, feel, experience, to communicate something not only about the artist

Giorgione (c. 1478–1510). The Tempest. c. 1505. Canvas, 30³/₄ × 28³/₈″. Accademia, Venice.

Titian (1485/90–1576). Homage to Venus. c. 1518. Canvas, 67³/₄ × 68⁷/₈″. The Prado, Madrid.

himself but, even more, about its own compelling, fascinating, illimitable inner life. We *enter into* such works rather than appreciate them from the outside as we do Early Renaissance art. They are part of us, we of them. The inexplicable subtlety of this new feeling—still "new" after 450 years—accounts for the need we feel to replace the too-demanding direct intuition of such art with biographical information, true or invented, about what the artist thought and, above all, felt. But of Giorgione we know almost nothing, of Titian too much. If we approach them through their biographies, it is equally impossible to grasp the message of a young man whose few years began and ended with as few traces as this tempest, and of the near centenarian heaped with honors and surfeited with travel. What matters is that each of them had an unsurpassed control over every element of composition, that each used light to model figures and settings with a richness of color which makes paint palpable, as if a sculptor had molded it in his hands, that a deep chord as of music resonates from the virile harmony of these hills and skies.

Titian. Venus with the Organist. 1548–50. Canvas, 45¼ × 82⅝″. State Museums, Berlin-Dahlem.

Titian. Christ Crowned with Thorns. c. 1570. Canvas, ▶ 9'2″ × 6'. Alte Pinakothek, Munich.

Titian, like all Venetians, took what he wanted from the Humanist return to Antique sources which was Florence's special province, and it turned out to be mostly an excuse for painting flesh, which he did superbly. In his *Homage to Venus* he takes the *putti* down from the pulpits and tombs they graced in Florence and lets them run wild—unspoiled children of nature. As for the *Venus with the Organist*, some writers would like to interpret it in terms of the Florentine Neo-Platonic notion of the Celestial Venus; it is, however, one of several such erotic pictures made for a gentleman's *camera privata*, in one of which the organist has been identified as the madrigal composer Girolamo Parabosco whose loose living scandalized even Venice. Here he may be Philip II of Spain. But Titian would not have been a man of his times had he lacked a darker strain in his character. The late *Crowning with Thorns* is an extraordinary image of the violence of the Passion. But the violence is less in the action than in the dramatic semidarkness lit by smoking torches, in the somberly glowing color, the highlighting of a few powerful patches of muscular anatomy, and most of all in the asymmetrical composition based not on geometrical shapes but on S-curves which slither up one body, flow into the next, intersect with or dissolve into others. As in the Early Renaissance (with Masaccio) and the High Renaissance (with Leonardo), the emotion is indeed contained in and expressed by motion, but here it is not by the motion of the individual figures—they seem arrested in mid-action—but by the motion permeating the entire canvas; not by gesture, then, but by composition.

While the rest of Italy braced itself against threats of war and heresy, Venice reveled in wealth, unruffled even when it became necessary for Fra Paolo Sarpi and the Doges to remind the Pope that Venice made its own politics and theology. The painter chosen to decorate its palaces and to portray its opulence was Veronese (two centuries later, in the giddy twilight of its decline, it would be Tiepolo, Guardi, and Canaletto). Veronese had left behind the minor masters of his native Verona and assimilated—with a truly Venetian appetite—the influences of Bellini and Mantegna, Correggio and Parmigianino, Raphael and Giulio Romano, and of course Titian. Yet it strains things to call him a Mannerist. There is too much sheer joy in reality and in the endless number of things he found he could do with paint. He is, simply, the Venetian *par excellence*. The creatures of Ovid's fables become, with him, well-nourished Venetian ladies picnicking on terra firma. Of the episodes of Christ's life, he by far preferred the Suppers. But he transformed them into Venetian banquets at which Christ was a guest of honor whose Biblical garments were, to say the least, inappropriate to the occasion. The patricians gorge themselves, the populace—Tartars, Turks, and Moors among them—look on in excitement, a horde of domestics serve the guests, dogs await scraps, and with shawms and gambas gentlemen

perform the latest airs, not of Cana but of the most musical city in late-Cinquecento Italy. The light is clear, the figures well defined, the setting a truncated triangle with a background of palaces from which the uninvited look on, the colors as sumptuous as satin, velvet, and brocades, the actions—what one would expect. The Inquisition did not approve, but what could it do with such a city and its favorite artist who couldn't see why, in a *Last Supper*, he should paint out a dog and paint in the Magdalen?

The minutes of the Tribunal of the Inquisition, Venice, July 18, 1573, with regard to the *Feast in the House of Simon* (now in the Accademia, Venice, and renamed, by order of the Inquisition, the *Feast in the House of Levi*—where Christ never dined). *Inquisitor:* In that *Supper* you painted for SS. Giovanni e Paolo, what is the significance of the man with a bleeding nose?

Paolo Veronese (1528–88). The Rape of Europa (detail). c. 1580. Canvas, total dimensions 7'10⁷/₈" × 9'9³/₄". Palazzo Ducale, Venice.

Paolo Veronese. The Marriage Feast at Cana (painted for the refectory of San Giorgio Maggiore, Venice). 1563. Canvas, 21′10¹/₄″ × 32′5³/₄″. The Louvre, Paris.

Veronese: I meant to portray a servant who had met with some accident. *I:* And those men-at-arms dressed as Germans, holding halberds? *V:* We painters take the same license as poets and jesters, so I introduced two halberdiers, one drinking, the other eating on the stairs close by. They are there in the service of the master of the house who, I am told, was a rich man and would have such servants. *I:* And the man dressed as a buffoon, holding on his wrist a parrot, why was he painted? *V:* For ornament, as is usual. *I:* Who sit at the table with Our Lord? *V:* The Twelve Apostles. *I:* What is Saint Peter, the first among them, doing? *V:* Carving the lamb to pass down to the other end of the table. *I:* What is the Apostle next to him doing? *V:* He holds up a dish to take what Saint Peter gives him. *I:* And what is the next one doing? *V:* He is using a toothpick to clean his teeth. *I:* Who do you think was really present at that Supper? *V:* I believe there was Christ with His Apostles. But if there is free space in a picture, I enrich it with other figures to fit the story. *I:* Are not the added decorations you painters use in pictures supposed to be fitting and proper to the subject and the main figures, or do you put them in for your own pleasure—simply whatever comes to your imagination without any discretion or judgment? *V:* I paint my pictures as I see fit and as well as my talent allows.

It is at best a half-truth to say that Venice was impervious to Mannerism. In Tintoretto it had the greatest, perhaps, of all Mannerist painters, precisely because he synthesized many elements from the art of his predecessors in Venice and elsewhere. The subjective drama, always latent in Titian, held in control by his implacable objectivity, bursts out in Tintoretto to imbue every component of painting—light, color, movement, space, composition—with the most intense dramatic energy. What is more, he fuses them together at such white heat that one cannot say what role in the drama is played by any one element: light, movement, space are as necessary to each other as Othello, Iago, and Desdemona to a tragedy whose fiery darkness has much in common with Tintoretto's art. Susanna is a great block of flesh rendered translucent by sunlight, but her meaning lies in the mysterious placement of the prying Elders along an axis leading into the far distance; without that background there would be beauty, yes, but not poetry. Even there, in open air, the lighting is theatrical. In the *Last Supper* there is no "background." There is only a tunnel of darkness without end,

Jacopo Tintoretto (1518–94). Susanna and the Elders. c. 1570. Canvas, $57^1/_2 \times 76''$. Kunsthistorisches Museum, Vienna.

Jacopo Tintoretto. The Last Supper. 1592–94. Canvas, 12′ × 18′8″. San Giorgio Maggiore, Venice.

which swallows up the personages strung along the table placed at an oblique angle to the picture frame, and the mouth of the tunnel is made up of a great horizontal oval sweeping from the kneeling woman in the foreground, through the servants and the wraiths of angels which seem to materialize from the smoking lamp, and around through the extended leg of the furthermost apostle. Space here is not a measurement, not an artifact of perspective, but a kind of infinite music marked by the resonant dark throbbing of the patches of color. The rhythm of that music is no more regular than that of the two great composers Lassus and Palestrina who died in the same year as Tintoretto. It is a psychological rhythm whose accents derive from intensity of expression, not from some *a priori* meter. From it there pours forth a whirlwind of nervous energy which has no caesura, not even at the glowing Christ who leans forward to administer the bread and wine of His body and blood. With Leonardo, Christ was a still center; here He is caught up in the force which sets the world spinning, and the angelic messengers converge on Him as if to veil the mystery in the instant which follows this. The very naturalism of the food and glittering utensils heightens the drama: light glints off their surfaces to create a subsidiary restlessness, and their naturalism is tense and disturbing, so unlike the robust acceptance of life by a Rubens or Bernini in the Baroque art that would follow. This, then, was the dark drama behind the sumptuous array of Veronese, the moral, spiritual, and emotional turmoil which would —which must—soon be engulfed in the brilliant self-assertion of the Baroque.

Luxurious objects like this, though made in Milan by craftsmen of many countries working together, came to be known as "Spanish style," no doubt because only the vast empire and trade of Spain could gather all the materials. Ebony came from tropical Asia and Africa, gold from the New World, rubies and pearls from the Far East, onyx for the cameos from
Saxony, South America,

and Hindustan, lapis lazuli from Russia and Afghanistan, emeralds from Russia, Africa, India, and South America; and from those same areas, with the addition of Japan, came the rock crystal. Duke Albrecht V paid six thousand scudi for it—an awesome sum which justified his installing the casket on an altar in the richly decorated chapel of his court at Munich.

Annibale Fontana (1540–87) with Milanese gem cutters and Munich or Augsburg cabinet-makers. The Albertina Casket. c. 1570. Ebony, rock crystal, enameled gold, lapis lazuli, onyx, cameos, rubies, emeralds, and pearls, $24^3/_8 \times 32^1/_4 \times 19^7/_8''$. Schatzkammer der Residenz, Munich.

Jacopo Sansovino (1486–1570). Palazzo Corner (Ca' Grande), Venice. Begun 1533.

Architecture in Venice was dominated for forty years by Sansovino, much as painting was by Titian. Putting behind him the sobriety of his native Florence and the stern grandeur of Rome (he too fled from the sack of the city in 1527), for Venice he created a style of open, airy buildings that wrote finis to whatever nostalgia the lagoon city may have had for its old Byzantine ways. The lower story of this palace is of rusticated stone, but it has nothing of the Florentines' austerity nor of Giulio Romano's fantasy. Instead it rises gently from the canal, and the balustrade above acts as a graceful transition to the upper stories which themselves are no more than a screen of windows (probably originally open loggias) from which the always-new view of the Canal Grande could be enjoyed. Decoration is held to a classical minimum—Venetian interiors were sumptuous enough—and the paired columns, brackets, and cornices all respect their functional purpose.

Alessandro Vittoria (1524–1608). Saint Jerome. 1565. Marble, height 6′2³/₄″. Santa Maria Gloriosa dei Frari, Venice.

ALEXANDER VICTORIA FACIEBAT

Sansovino was noteworthy as a sculptor also, and his only peer was Vittoria. A true Venetian, Vittoria made warmly modeled statues of great solidity whose multiple surfaces are designed to catch and reflect the clear bright light of Venice. The ultimate source of his style was Michelangelo and especially the *Dying Slave* which he studied thoroughly, though he could know it only from engravings, the two *Slaves* having been sent off so soon to France. From it he learned continuity of movement, how to make plastic planes interlock and flow into each other without interruption of energy—a lesson which, in the Baroque, Bernini would carry to new heights. Vittoria is even more notable for his portrait busts in which superbly realistic, warm-blooded likenesses are infused with grandeur by the energy of the modeling.

Andrea Palladio (1508–80). Villa Rotonda, near Vicenza. Begun 1550, completed in 1606 by Vincenzo Scamozzi (1552–1616).

Quietly, with never a hint of extravagance, our period closes with the serene architecture of Palladio. Of immense intelligence, a humble stonecutter schooled by the Humanist epic poet–playwright–architect Trissino, Palladio not only purified the architecture of his time of all nonessentials but also wrote down his ideas in a manner so clear, so "Palladian," that his treatise became the architects' bible through the eighteenth century and, in our age of functionalism, has become so again. With Palladio we come full circle, back to the rational precepts of Alberti and, past him, to Vitruvius. His palaces, churches, and villas are constructed according to those ratios of musical proportions that Pythagoras said governed the universe and that Alberti and Brunelleschi had sensed. He conceived exteriors and interiors as a single harmony and in concord with the natural setting about them. Such noble serenity is Greek, not Roman, and Palladio rejected all the rich vocabulary of architectural ornament to arrive at the purity of the Villa Rotonda, a country house at once grand and simple, a perfectly symmetrical central-plan structure of four temple porticoes interlocking into the perfect square of the core of the building. Beauty and commodiousness according to the measure of man had been the first ideal of the Renaissance; with Palladio they became the ultimate achievement of Mannerism.

It is appropriate that Palladio's last project should have been the Teatro Olimpico. Completed after his death in 1580 by Scamozzi, it was opened on Sunday, March 3, 1585 with Sophocles' *Oedipus Tyrannus*, the first Greek tragedy—after almost two centuries of Humanism—to be staged in an Italian translation respectful of the text and with the choruses sung *all'antica* (composed by Andrea Gabrieli, organist at San Marco in Venice). The three thousand spectators reputed to have crammed the theater for the première were aware of the solemnity of the occasion. Theatrical activity had been rich throughout the Renaissance, and the dramatized *feste* that took place in public squares on state occasions were perhaps the fullest expression of the age, though—alas!—the least durable. But in the Teatro Olimpico the dream of a permanent theater was realized, and most nobly in the *frons scenae*, the fixed stage setting in burnished wood with stucco statues. One great triumphal arch and four lesser openings afford views of "streets" leading off to infinity by highly ingenious perspective foreshortening of the fully-constructed house façades lining them. And here too was Palladio's and Mannerism's other triumph: to make a solid reality of the dream of perspective that had haunted Uccello and that some artist in Urbino had set down in paint as a hope for an ideal city.

Andrea Palladio and Vincenzo Scamozzi. Interior, Teatro Olimpico, Vicenza. 1580–85.

In 1528 Charles V put a temporary stop to work on Diego da Siloe's design for the cathedral of Granada: it was "*a lo romano*," he complained, and jarred with the adjacent Gothic Capilla Real begun in 1505 as a tomb for Ferdinand and Isabella. Yet the two styles had been coexisting happily in Spain for almost a century, and Spain's artistic culture was fully cosmopolitan: Jan van Eyck had been there in 1427, Spaniards acquired works by Rogier van der Weyden and other Flemings before Italy suspected their existence, artists from Burgundy, Flanders, France, and Italy worked side by side with Spaniards and usually settled there for life, and promising talents were sent to study in Italy and the Low Countries. As early as the 1440s Luis Dalmau painted altarpieces with all the realism and precision of the Flemings. In 1490 Bartolomé Bermejo signed a *Pietà* whose vast panoramic landscape not only embraces the figures but echoes their passionate grief as did few Italian landscapes of the time; what is more, the portrait of the unkempt, unshaven mourning donor has a psychological insight rarely matched in all of art. If the nude is rare, this is Spanish *pudor*, not a refusal of the Renaissance's human element, and would remain so in Spanish art. The native tradition in sculpture had already assimilated the Burgundian Gothic style. It was enriched around 1500 by Andrea Sansovino, Torrigiani, and others who brought the lessons of Donatello, Pollaiuolo, Mino da Fiesole, and Leonardo. In architecture the collaboration of Spaniards, foreign-trained Spaniards, and foreigners resulted in Gothic buildings with Renaissance ornament, Renaissance structures with Gothic motifs, then the uniquely Spanish "Plateresque" style, and finally great palaces more severely classicistic than anything in Italy. The reaction set in early against the Gothic. The forms it assumed were not those of the Italian Renaissance, however, but native inventions, chief among them the *plateresco*, a florid decorative style in which stone was treated as if it were malleable as silver (*plata*). Like the abstract geometrical *mudéjar* style of interior wall and ceiling decoration, it was Moorish in origin and therefore native to Spain. It is often argued that Spain did not participate in the Renaissance because it did not adopt Greco-Roman forms. But those forms belonged to Italy, and wherever they appeared outside of Italy it was always as an importation. Spain drew on its own antique tradition, the Moresque, and soon found the way to apply it to buildings conceived as a harmonious unity, stressing horizontals in Renaissance manner rather than Gothic perpendiculars. If the great cathedrals continued to

be built in Gothic style, they were in France too (and the largest Flamboyant Gothic church in the world is the Milan cathedral of the fifteenth and sixteenth centuries). It is often claimed now that the Humanist rediscovery of Antiquity was not decisive for the Italian Renaissance; both the merit and weakness of that argument can be deduced from the fact that Spain, where Humanist studies were not encouraged, where Erasmus was judged heretical, had nothing really like the Italian Renaissance but, nevertheless, had its own native "rebirth," so much the less needed because of the great achievements of Spanish Gothic in all fields. The impulsion came first from the *Reyes Católicos* Ferdinand and Isabella, from their desire to affirm the "Spanishness" of the nation freed from the Moors. The accession of Charles V, Hapsburg emperor and King of

Spain, brought new horizons, new tasks, new influences—those of Titian and Leone Leoni above all, though neither set foot in Spain. For Charles they created an "Imperial" style appropriate to the moral dignity of the vast new empire—terse, austere, virile, with a sober yet sensual fire beneath the surface, as there was with the King himself. There is much of the Counter Reformation in this art, but also much of the new conception of the Nation as contrasted with the ingrown, preciously cultured art of the Italian principalities and cities. For courts abroad and at home, the grandeur of a great empire held up a new ideal and new goals. Philip II, obsessed with great sins and greater repentance, bought for himself Titian's nude Venuses and Bosch's infernal nightmares, but from architecture he demanded classical monumentality, and he gave his favor to the new international style of court portraiture of the Netherlander Anthonis Mor and his Spanish follower Coëllo, with its regal costumes and poses conforming to the rigorous new court etiquette.

◄ Leone Leoni (1509–90). Mary of Austria, Queen of Hungary, Sister to Charles V. 1553. Bronze, height 65³/₈″. The Prado, Madrid.

Alonso Sánchez Coëllo (1531/32–88). Elizabeth of Valois, Queen of Spain, Wife to Philip II. Canvas, 64¹/₈ × 36″. Kunsthistorisches Museum, Vienna.

The Plateresque style is based on a profusion of ornamentation such as we have found only at the Certosa of Pavia, and the craftsmen from France or the Netherlands who worked on this façade may have known the Lombard style, if only from sketchbooks. But the Plateresque is uniquely Spanish in its use of broken curves and countercurves, flattened elliptical arches, fluted or twisted columns, roundels with portrait heads, coats of arms, and emphasis on abstract design rather than figurative sculpture. The varied motifs are tightly compressed into a screen of relief carving laid over a flat façade, very much like the huge carved retable, the wall of sculpture rising to the entire height of the sanctuary behind the main altar in Spanish churches.

As Holy Roman Emperor, Charles V was not averse to rivaling Rome itself. His palace in Granada, designed by a Spaniard trained in Italy, owes much to the imposing *palazzi* Bramante and Raphael built in Rome. But for all that its immense circular courtyard recalls the Colosseum, it is Spanish: in a country where drops of water are precious, it was common to build circular courts sloping down to a catch-basin well.

With Philip II, Gothic fantasy was ruled out, Plateresque exuberance banished to the American colonies, and rigorous classicism—already so impressively advanced by his father's palace—was made the ideal goal of Spanish architecture for two centuries to come. The Escorial is more than a palace: it is a complex containing a royal palace, a monastery, a pantheon for the dead kings, and an enormous church which forms the core. It has 670 feet of grim gray granite frontage, ascetically bare of decoration, and it contains over four thousand rooms built around sixteen courts. The gridiron plan may come from Filarete's Ospedale Maggiore in Milan, but it is more Spanish—more quixotic—than that: at the battle of Saint-Quentin, Philip

Juan Bautista de Toledo (d. 1567) and Juan de Herrera (c. 1530–97). The Escorial. 1563–82.

Pedro Machuca (active 1517–50). Inner court, Palace of Charles V, The Alhambra, Granada. 1527–68.

vowed to build a monument to the saint on whose day Spain triumphed, Saint Lawrence, and he decreed that the plan must imitate the grill on which the saint was burned for his faith—these were the times of Saint Theresa of Avila and Saint John of the Cross. But El Greco, the only artist capable of painting such mystic ecstasy, a Greek transplanted to Venice, was not yet in Spain; and so Philip called from Italy the Mannerists Tibaldi, Cambiaso, and Federico Zuccari to decorate this grandiose dream of a king. Isolated, forbidding, a sanctuary dedicated to the apotheosis of dead kings and a living one, but centered on the Church from which he drew his divine right, the Escorial somehow strangely recalls the sacred city of Moctezuma, another emperor who believed to the end that kingship and divinity were one.

Alonso Berruguete (1485/89–1561). Christ on the Cross, detail of the retable of San Benito el Real. 1527–32. Polychromed wood, height 5′10⁷/₈″.. Museo Nacional de Escultura, Valladolid.

Except for tombs and portrait busts, sculpture was in polychromed wood, painted over gold leaf to heighten both the luster and the dramatic effect. Often described as "realistic," Spanish sculpture is anything but that. It is dramatic, theatrical, violent in gesture and expression, without repose, distorted with passion, but never realistic. Even Florentines like Andrea Sansovino who came to Spain could not alter this (in France the Italians imposed their own style, in Spain they capitulated before the national style). Though Berruguete had worked under Michelangelo, he profited more from Rosso and Pontormo whose extreme expressionism was closer to the native Spanish religious passion. His figures are elongated, drawn out as if made of some plastic material, their poses weirdly balletic, their faces grim masks of almost medieval stylization—in brief, an extreme form of anticlassical, psychological Mannerism. Yet, for all their exacerbated refinement, they are faithful to a folk tradition. So too are those of a younger contemporary, Juan de Juni from Joigny in Champagne but thoroughly assimilated to Spain despite the Italian influence he may have undergone at Fontainebleau. Juni's figures are squat, contorted, writhing in movement, paroxysmal in grief, and their gilded polychrome catches the light

Domingo Beltrán (1535–90). Christ on the Cross. Polychromed wood. Hermitage of Los Doctrinos, Alcalá de Henares.

of flickering candles so that they seem to move jerkily in their anguish. A generation later, under Philipp II, Beltrán's figures are clothed in mortal flesh and their grief is mortal. The stylized features of Berruguete's Christ are the quintessence of suffering, and His wasted arms struggle against death. Beltrán's Christ is resigned, the entire body weight hangs limp, the head sinks in calm resignation. This is in no way a matter of "improved" technique—the earlier Spanish sculptors handled their craft with even greater virtuosity than the later ones—but of a general submission to the grip of the Counter Reformation which sought to bridle individual passion into safer ways (as in Italy with Cambiaso and Zuccari who, significantly enough, were among the painters Philip chose for the Escorial). This was the climate for a different art, one of controlled fire and stern majesty as represented by Leone Leoni and his son Pompeo (who settled in Spain), sculptors who belonged to, or created, an aristocratic art which, in the Baroque, would increasingly fuse with the popular tradition to create a style in which devout sentiment won out over passion.

Even painters who, directly or indirectly, came under foreign influence—Fernando Yáñez de la Almedina, Vicente Juan Macip, Juan de Juanes, Pedro Machuca—transformed the lessons of Raphael, Leonardo, and the Netherlanders into a passionate expression which deserves the name of Mannerism, even when it was a Mannerism before the fact, a native Spanish trait. Movement is more intense, composition more tortuous, colors harsher and more dramatically contrasted, details rendered with a naturalism more Netherlandish than Italian. With Alonso Berruguete, as great a painter as a sculptor, the terrible, compelling, inward character of Pontormo and Rosso found a home more natural to it than intellectualistic Florence. The spectral, slightly mad personages of Pedro de Campaña (Pieter de Kempeneer, originally of Brussels), Luis de Morales' Madonnas swooning in a haze of *sfumato* and haggard Christs crushed by the Cross, the nocturnal Venetian dramas of the saints by Juan Fernández de Navarrete ("El Mudo"—he was deaf), all added other facets to an art which, by reason of its own inner tensions, would inevitably explode into the unworldly visions of El Greco. One can repeat the easy platitude that El Greco was unique, without precedent, a Byzantine intruder into a Western world, only by ignoring all the Spanish art that came before him and his own personal development. The works he did during eleven years in Venice give little hint that he would ever be more than a gifted follower of Titian, Tintoretto, and Jacopo Bassano. Suddenly, with his arrival in Spain in 1577, ecstasy suffuses his earth-bound Venetian style, the figures soar, burn, suffer, become fractured by hallucinatory light, shattered by the strain of the effort to transcend both gravity and the artist's visionary genius. The world in which they are, but do not truly exist, is lit by phosphorescent colors which those angelic visitants could only have brought with them from the outermost spheres. Is this transmutation of all the painters' values merely accidental, something thought of on the road from Venice to Toledo? The answer is crystal clear: neither Venetian sensuousness, Roman grandeur, nor Florentine refinement could equip the Cretan, who had been trained in the art of the icon, with more than the tools of his craft. Spain, with its visionary religious art, liberated him, at once, from all the constraints of Byzantium and from the burden of the alien Italian tradition. In Spain he found both his spiritual and his artistic home, and his art stems from Spain's as surely as Raphael's from Perugino's, and as Michelangelo's from Signorelli's.

Domenico Theotocopoulos, known as El Greco (1541–1614). Assumption of the Virgin. c. 1608. Canvas, 10'8" × 5'6⁷/₈". Museo de Santa Cruz, Toledo.

El Greco. The Grand Inquisitor ▶ Cardinal Don Fernando Nino de Guevara. c. 1598. Canvas, 76³/₈ × 51¹/₄". Metropolitan Museum of Art, New York.

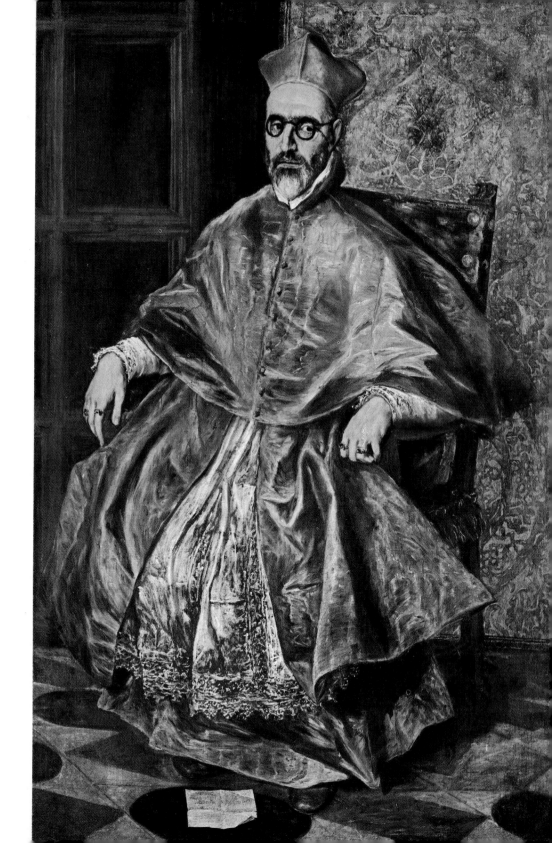

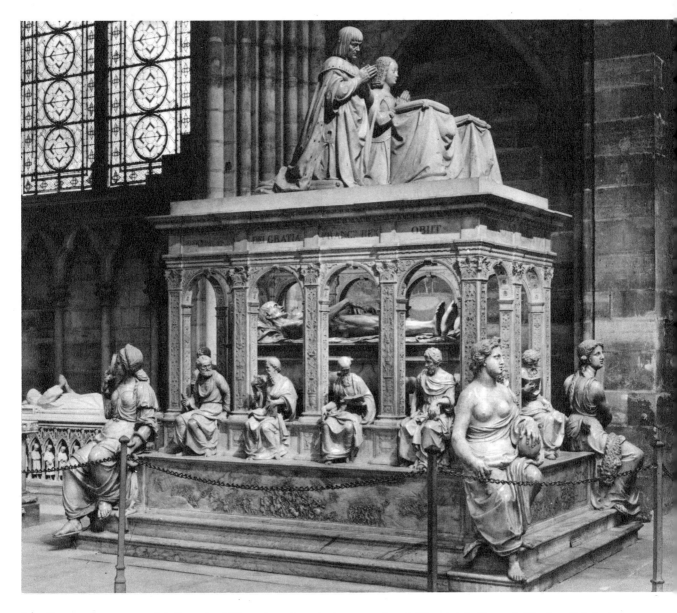

◄ Jean Fouquet (c. 1415–c. 1480). Portrait of King Charles VII of France. c. 1452–53. Panel, 33⁷/₈ × 28³/₈″. The Louvre, Paris.

Antonio (1479–1519) and Giovanni (1485–1549) Giusti, called Juste. Tomb of Louis XII and Anne of Britany. 1515–31. Marble. Abbey Church of St.-Denis, Paris.

FRANCE No other country has ever achieved the glorious feat of France's unbroken hegemony, through a half-millennium of Romanesque and Gothic, over all the arts except perhaps painting, in which the miniature and tapestry took the place occupied, in Italy, by Giotto and Simone Martini (France gained little from Simone's stay in Avignon). That is why, when Masaccio, Piero della Francesca, and Brunelleschi were breaking the bonds of the International Gothic style to win to a new classical conception of life and art, when Jan van Eyck and Rogier van der Weyden were pinning reality to a dissecting

Central façade, Château of Chambord, original design by Domenico da Cortona (1470–1545) subsequently modified. c. 1519–c. 1540.

Staircase, François I wing, ▶ Château of Blois. 1515–24.

board to examine its every wrinkle, France remained happily at that highest point of exquisite elegance which Huizinga described as "the waning of the Middle Ages." A few painters, like Fouquet, returned from Italy with a hint of perspective, a new way of painting draperies and modeling figures, but even on large panels they remained miniaturists. From their incursions into the Peninsula, Charles VIII, Louis XII, and François I learned of the Renaissance, almost a century old by then, but what they admired and imitated was the "Gothic" Certosa of Pavia, not the "classical" Palazzo Rucellai. When they began to build new palaces such as Chambord, there was a new simplicity, true, a certain stress on the horizontal, and a ground plan like that of Poggio a Caiano, but the roof was still crowned with a tangle of pinnacles, turrets, dormers, and tower-tall chimneys resembling one of those enchanted woods through which knights hunted damsels in France's medieval epics of chivalry. Even when a school of painting developed at Fontainebleau, its figures—however inspired by

Italian models—were still the willowy, nerveless creatures of the International Gothic, though their brocaded garments were left by some forest fountain and they disported themselves in Italianate nudity. Because the Renaissance represented a modern way of life in which rulers competed for prestige not only on the battlefield but also at the banqueting table and in council halls, the monarchy took drastic steps to overcome resistance to the new style. For the tomb of his parents, a major undertaking certain to have an impact on the general taste, François I engaged the Giusti brothers. Adapting a Lombard tradition, they created the typical French royal tomb in which the kings lie naked in death within a freestanding chapel-like structure on whose roof they are seen again, this time dressed as in life and kneeling at prayer, as "*priants.*" Where Burgundian tombs traditionally had surrounded the defunct with weeping attendants, "*pleurants,*" here the Giusti placed statues of the Apostles and the Virtues, perhaps a reminiscence of Michelangelo's first project for the tomb of Julius II. But the "*gisants,*" the naked dead pair, still seem Gothic in their stark naturalism

(even the incisions and sutures made in embalming are rendered, and the teeth are bared in *rigor mortis*) and these, it has been proposed, may be by the Frenchman Michel Colombe. If François hoped for immediate results, there were few: the exactly contemporary tomb of Cardinal d'Amboise in Rouen has somewhat more human figures, but they are set in a Gothic framework which, in comparison, would make a Plateresque retable seem sober. At his château of Blois, François attempted to incorporate Renaissance elements into an existing medieval castle with odd but fascinating results, not helped by the unfamiliarity of the builders with problems solved long before in Italy. Startlingly beautiful as the exterior spiral staircase is, it differs from those of the fifteenth century in France mainly in its decoration; but it does have a monumentality, a sense of structure within space, which is Renaissance.

Jean Clouet (active 1516–40/41).
Portrait of François I. c. 1535. Panel,
37³/₄ × 29″. The Louvre, Paris.

Blois's plan lacks the classical balance of the Renaissance because the existing foundations were used. Its roof is steeply pitched, as were and would be all roofs in northern climates, its windows are still tall and mullioned. But its ornamental motifs do have a Renaissance distinction (though many are nineteenth-century reconstructions), and one façade is made up of loggias that are an awkward if well-intentioned effort to copy Bramante's loggias in the Vatican. All in all, it is an imaginative design with a fantasy and elegance which already point to something indigenously French. The King himself was the epitome of such elegance, and this his court painter, Jean Clouet of Brussels, caught superbly with a Netherlandish eye for the dashing character of the man and for the fine detail of his splendid attire. François saw clearly that the old, fortress-like castles would no longer do for the amenities of a new kind of court life centered around the person of an attractive and generous king. His reasons were not a matter of taste but of policy: it was a way of keeping an eye on ambitious rival nobles. After his return in 1525 from imprisonment in Italy and Spain, he set about enlarging the medieval hunting lodge at Fontainebleau into a great palace. Once again it was impossible to conceive a unified plan, but this time economy resulted in a simplification in structure and decoration which has come to be called "classical" and which reached its apogee more than a century later when Louis XIV refused Bernini's design for the Louvre and, again, when he projected his own gilded cage for restless nobles at Versailles. Compared with the *palazzi* we have seen, this new-found simplicity may still seem extravagant, but it represents the first outright victory of the French over the seductions of their own Flamboyant Gothic and is, indeed, French and not Italian. One senses the struggle between old and new in this façade. It was too early to hope for the classically ordered symmetry of the palace front as practiced in Italy from Alberti to Bramante and beyond, or for the Roman majesty of Charles V's palace in Granada built in the same years: the Fontainebleau façade seems to sprawl to its sides, held together only by the focal point of the wonderfully imaginative, swirling Mannerist staircase added by Jean Du Cerceau in 1634. The flanking towers are spaced at irregular intervals, there is no grasp of harmony through balance in either the lower or upper stories, the mullioned windows betray the native fondness for the Gothic in their perpendicular lines accentuated by dormers, chimneys, and steep-pitched roofs. The wall surfaces, however, are decorated only by the pure lines of flat pilasters set against a smooth plastered wall. Fontainebleau grew like a plant, sending out shoots in all directions and in all styles as the King and his builders added wing after wing, seeking to incorporate all the novelties from Italy and to profit from the presence in France of Serlio and Primaticcio. In shaking off Gothic disorder, François and his artists simply bypassed the classical equilibrium of the High Renaissance and plunged into the quite different world of Mannerism, whose exacerbated refinement, valuation of decoration above function, hypersensitivity, and intellectual preciosity were destined to leave their mark on every aspect of French culture for centuries to come.

Gilles le Breton (active 1527–52), attributed. Entrance court (Cour du Cheval Blanc), Fontainebleau. 1528–40.

Rosso Fiorentino and assistants. The Gallery of François I, Fontainebleau. c. 1533–40. Decoration in fresco, stucco, gilding, and wood paneling.

Early in his reign François had attempted to make the great leap forward by enticing to France the greatest masters of the High Renaissance. Andrea del Sarto came briefly only, Leonardo da Vinci lurked around the court like a dying Merlin and did nothing, Michelangelo refused. Those who came afterward were some of the brightest luminaries of the early generations of Mannerism—Rosso, Primaticcio, Luca Penni, Niccolò Dell'Abbate, Francesco Salviati, Sebastiano Serlio, Cellini. For François and his successors they created the *École de Fontainebleau*, a French art whose practitioners were Italian and in which we can only guess at the authorship of the few works attributed to Frenchmen (though in the provinces, far from Fontainebleau, a few well-defined French personalities can be made out). What is extraordinary is that in many ways those Italians did indeed become French, that they forged a style so sympathetic to the national character that we forget that no Frenchman played more than a supernumerary's role in it until its very end. Even the fiery,

Francesco Primaticcio (1504–70). Ulysses and Penelope. c. 1545. Canvas, 45$\frac{1}{4}$ × 48$\frac{3}{8}$″. The Toledo Museum of Art. Gift of Edward D. Libbey.

imaginative Florentine radical Rosso became a decorator and created the first royal gallery, a long, elaborately decorated corridor to be used for festivities and state occasions. Its decoration (altered by time, the whims of kings, and the incompetence of restorers) is unprecedented. Based on a complex literary program of glorification of François as leader in war and learning, it comprises a series of painted panels set into the walls (an innovation) above finely carved wooden wainscoting. Each panel is framed by stucco statuary, in the round and in relief, subtly related in theme to the paintings, a stunning tangle of long-limbed erotic nudes, garlands, animals, *putti*, strapwork, and cartouches (some frames are merely painted in *trompe l'oeil* to look like statuary). Nothing is static, nothing regular. Everything is designed to delight and surprise—the familiar formula of *fare piacere, fare stupore.*

Francesco Primaticcio. Lunette above door, Porte Dorée wing, Fontainebleau. 1528–40. Stucco.

Francesco Primaticcio. Apelles painting Campaspe. c. 1541–45. ▶ Oval fresco framed by stucco statues and decoration. Chamber of the Duchesse d'Étampes, Fontainebleau.

Neither Rosso nor Primaticcio lost his native strangeness at Fontainebleau, the sense of figures struggling or lost in an indeterminate space. But mysticism gave way to eroticism, expressionism to play of fancy. For this, Primaticcio was well prepared—he had worked under Giulio Romano at the Palazzo del Tè. With the silky textures of his restrained palette, amorous dalliance becomes cool, self-possessed, all traces of Italianate earthiness refined away in the diffused light and moist atmosphere of the Île-de-France.

Francesco Primaticcio. Grotto of the Pines, Fontainebleau. c. 1543.

Bernard Palissy (c. 1510–90). Oval plate in ► "*rustique*" style. Polychrome ceramic, length 20$^1/_2$". The Louvre, Paris.

In France the "minor" arts have always kept pace with the "major" arts. No wonder then that the Fontainebleau style was taken up by native craftsmen even before native artists were goaded to emulation. In the remotest provinces, artisans came to know the new motifs through engravings done after Rosso's and Primaticcio's drawings and from pattern books by Étienne Delaune, René Boyvin, and Hugues Sambin. Elongated figures in swooning poses appeared in stained-glass windows. Armoires and chairs were carved with allegorical nudes, chimerical beasts, *grotteschi*, and strapwork. For vitreous enameling on metal plaques, an art practiced especially in Limoges, designs had always been taken from engravings: in the early 1500s the Pénicauds copied their religious subjects from Schongauer and Dürer; then, in 1535, Léonard Limousin used a mythological subject by Raphael, and his rivals promptly set about collecting the engravings after drawings by the masters that Marcantonio Raimondi was turning out in Rome, though they held back from the Fontainebleau style until around 1560. The contact was more direct in another art: the King had all the decoration of his just-finished gallery copied in a set of tapestries. In 1518 Girolamo della Robbia had introduced faïence and majolica, and that new art gave us the strangest by-product of the School of Fontainebleau, the ceramics of Bernard Palissy.

There was published at Venice in 1499 the oddest, most beautiful, most influential book of the Renaissance, the *Hypnerotomachia Poliphili* by—perhaps—the monk Francesco Colonna. It recounts a dream so bizarre, so cryptic, so erotic that in our time it has been subjected to Jungian psychoanalysis. Its woodcut illustrations, attributed to the school of Mantegna, and its minute descriptions of ruins, fountains, Antique temples, pleasure groves, and hieroglyphical inscriptions furnished countless new motifs to artists, and both Renaissance and Mannerism are inconceivable without that strange freight of imagery. In 1546 it was published in French

with woodcuts ascribed to Jean Goujon based on the Italian originals. Among its weird settings are haunted rocky grottoes suggestive of more than meets the eye. These were imitated at Mantua by Giulio Romano, in Florence by Giambologna and Buontalenti, at Fontainebleau by Primaticcio (with giants materializing out of rusticated blocks), and finally twice in Paris by Bernard Palissy, an eccentric, highly erudite maker of ceramics from southern France who died at eighty in the Bastille, condemned as a Huguenot. A passionate naturalist, he gave public lectures on fossils, wrote treatises on ceramic techniques and on everything else he knew about, and invented the "*rustique*" style in which casts from nature of snakes, fish, beetles, snails, lizards, and plants were incorporated into his plates and vessels. Palissy himself tells us where he got his fantastic inspirations: at the bottom of the pool in his grotto he put ceramic fish so designed that the movement of the water made them appear to wriggle—a trick described in the *Hypnerotomachia* and one worthy of the cunning artificers of illusion in the palace at Fontainebleau.

With the rise of a new merchant class, private dwellings too became more opulent and comfortable, and the *hôtels*, so characteristic of French cities, copied in a more intimate manner the great châteaux of the nobles. This *hôtel* was built for Nicolas Le Valois d'Écoville, reputed to be an alchemist and, if so, a highly successful one, since he was the richest man in Normandy. Built by a local master mason, it uses the new forms in a provincial adaptation. The eye is carried steeply upward by superimposed Corinthian columns (in France the more chaste Doric and Ionic orders never found much favor) which frame classicistic statuary. There is still a certain tightness in the façade, though the windows are pleasantly large.

The years 1540–41 were the turning point: Serlio was brought from Italy, the Frenchman Philibert Delorme returned from his studies there. Serlio's illustrated handbook showed architects what had been built in Italy and explained in clear, nontheoretical terms how to do the same. Already more free, more inclined to the picturesque than his compatriots, Serlio soon came under the charm of France. At Ancy-le-Franc, built for the Grand Master of the Waters and Forests of France, brother-in-law to Diane de Poitiers, Serlio's design changed in the course of work from a virile *castello* to a graceful, livable, commodious château in a style we have come to think of as purely French (though today still the French find Ancy-le-Franc too austerely symmetrical). As so often in Italy and France alike, the simplicity of the exterior is countered by the lavishness of the interior decoration which was confided to Primaticcio and Niccolò Dell'Abbate, Serlio's associates at Fontainebleau.

Philibert Delorme (c. 1510–70) and Pierre Bontemps (1505/10–68). Tomb of François I and Claude of France. Begun 1547. Marble. Abbey Church of St.-Denis, Paris.

Death came for François I, the king who had dreamed of a Renaissance to rival Italy's and had even married off his son to Catherine, the great-granddaughter of Lorenzo de' Medici. His tomb, designed by Delorme, with *gisants* and bas-reliefs by Bontemps, closed his life in a Roman triumph, with a classicizing adaptation of the Giusti's tomb for his predecessor. But the sovereigns in prayer display a new devoutness, and the

Ligier Richier (c. 1500–66/67), attributed. Tomb of René de Châlons. After 1544. Marble. St.-Pierre, Bar-le-Duc (Meuse).

tomb has a monumental sobriety more typical of the morose, hyperdevout young Henri II than of the *vieux galant* who wrote to Diane de Poitiers that he had never had other than "a single God, a single mistress." Death, and even religion, had never been much of a spoilsport at Fontainebleau, but among the bourgeoisie and in the provinces Luther's and Calvin's doctrines were winning converts (François's sister Marguerite had made of her kingdom of Navarre a hotbed of the new heresy). Copies of the *Ars moriendi*—the Art of Graceful Dying—were well thumbed by the populace, and Holbein's *Dance of Death* woodcuts were published in Lyons, reaching ten editions in twelve years. The life-sized sculptured Depositions on church altars, which were traditional in the provinces, took on a new dramatic character in which Gothic naturalism was made more moving by Renaissance lifelikeness. In the Duchy of Lorraine to the east, the new

religious convictions made headway, and to their stern message of mortal vanity must be due this macabre funeral monument in which an *écorché*—a body stripped of skin with muscles and bones exposed—proclaims in an extravagant gesture, dead heart in hand, the corruption of the flesh. No such grim sermon penetrated the barriers which protected the capital and the court from contact with life—and death.

In sculpture the purest expression of the period is that of Jean Goujon, who had ample opportunity to learn from Cellini in France but never saw Italy before he fled there, as a Huguenot refugee, soon before his death. With him the last traces of Gothic excess are cast off to arrive at something almost unique in the Renaissance, a style having more to do with classical Greece than with Imperial Rome. His Fountain of the Innocents, inaugurated on the occasion of the new king Henri II's triumphal entry into Paris, is known now only in the truncated form to which the Neoclassical eighteenth century reduced it, but its original design was illustrated in the treatise of Serlio (to whom some writers ascribe it) and has no resemblance to the Hindu-like temple we see today. Fortunately its nine relief panels have been preserved, and these are models of classical perfection, their sensitive modeling showing full comprehension of Cellini's most mature Mannerist style. The nymph seen here is a superb adaptation of flowing draperies to a nude Thetis drawn by Rosso and engraved by Caraglio, while another clearly derives from a Roman statue of Eros. Even more extraordinary is the Tribune of the Caryatids made for a hall in the new Louvre. How did a stay-at-home French sculptor come to know about the caryatids of Antiquity? Vitruvius described them, the Italians engraved them, but more important were the casts of Antique and Renaissance statues that Primaticcio brought back from the trip to Rome he made around 1540 at the command of François who wished to make available to French artists the great treasures of the past and present which Italy had in such abundance. Whatever Goujon

Jean Goujon. Fontaine des Innocents (present state after complete alteration in the 18th century). 1547–49. Paris.

◄ Jean Goujon (1510/14–c. 1568). Tribune of the Caryatids. 1550–51 (figures somewhat altered in the 19th century). Marble, height of figures 11′5³/₄″. The Louvre, Paris.

Jean Goujon. Nymph. Marble relief on the Fontaine des Innocents, Paris. ▼

learned from them, and it was much, he transformed into images of ideal feminine beauty whose gentle grace and almost abstract perfection make of them the very finest expressions of a Mannerism which, with him, became at last truly French.

Henri II's great project was the Louvre. The threat of civil war brought the court back to the capital, with effects—good and bad—on the arts. The new palace was a strictly French undertaking in the new period of national consciousness, and native architects were at last equipped for such a large-scale work. Lescot knew Italy only through books of engravings and that

147

Pierre Lescot (c. 1500/15–78). The Square Court (Cour Carrée), Palace of the Louvre, Paris. Begun 1546.

St.-Étienne-du-Mont, Paris. Choir completed c. 1538; choir screen, ▶ attributed to Philibert Delorme, completed c. 1545.

may explain the intimate character of this façade. It is large but not monumental, as if the architect had aspired to something very grand but, lacking a firsthand acquaintance with the great palaces of the Renaissance, had succeeded only in transferring a drawing into stone. The three arches are not "triumphal" because their horizontal interval is too narrow for their height, and the repetition of three similar structures means that there is no scale by which to measure grandeur. There is a certain unfamiliarity with that which makes the organic strength of a building, so windows, fluted Corinthian pilasters, pediments, moldings, friezes, niches, freestanding statues, reliefs all crowd in on one another with a concentrated pressure we associate with the extremes of Mannerist nervous instability. And yet, the details are sensitive and beautiful, and Goujon's sculptured decoration is in full harmony with Lescot's architectural idea. The Church resisted the new style much longer, and the few attempts do little more than overlay Gothic exuberance with Renaissance motifs. The openwork spiral staircase of the choir screen of St.-Étienne-du-Mont has a fantastic elegance which, some feel, could only come from France's finest architect, Philibert Delorme.

One of the first acts, and the first scandals, of Henri II's reign was to deed the château of Chenonceau to Diane de Poitiers, *Grande Seneschale de France*, once his father's mistress and now, aging, his. As beauty waned, avarice grew, and her shameless passion for wealth was something no one could satisfy better than the King. Chenonceau was built around 1515 for a rich bourgeois by local masons who made it one of the most beautiful châteaux of France, a fairy-tale castle. When Diane acquired it, she engaged Delorme to build a bridge from the castle to the opposite bank (her consistent patronage of Delorme was the noblest act of her career). Upon Henri's death, his queen, Catherine de' Medici, took a ladylike revenge for years of humiliation: Chenonceau was returned to the crown, the money-mad ex-beauty was banished from the court, and packed off to the rather grimly medieval château of Chaumont. Catherine then had Jean Bullant or, some say, a certain Denis Courtin build a three-storied gallery over Delorme's bridge.

Little remains of Diane's own château of Anet except the chapel and the entrance gate seen here (the central portion of the façade was removed to the courtyard of the École des Beaux-Arts in Paris). But the entrance is enough to show that Delorme understood what Lescot, in the Louvre, did not: how to let a struc-

◄ Château of Chenonceau. 1515–22. Bridge added 1556–59 by Philibert Delorme; gallery above it added c. 1580, possibly on a design by Jean Bullant (c. 1520/25–78).

Philibert Delorme. Entrance portal, Château of Anet. c. 1552.

ture "breathe" by juxtaposing flat walls with architectonic elements which are both decorative and functional—in this case Doric columns, a frieze of triglyphs and metopes, segmented arches, and the graceful openwork balustrades. The result is that monumentality which can only be achieved through simplicity. It is, moreover, unique and entirely original. There is nothing similar in France or Italy. Any hint of sternness was cleverly avoided by contrasting the masonry with two pieces of bronze sculpture: the stag and hounds which move at the striking of the hours, and Cellini's lunette of Diana (the original is now in the Louvre). Though Cellini designed the lunette to surmount the entrance to Fontainebleau, it was one of Henri's many gifts to Diane after his father's death, and it seemed not to trouble him that the bronze goddess was embracing a stag, one of François's heraldic emblems. In any case, the incredibly elongated figure is exactly right above the door at Anet, a horizontal line parallel to the main lines of the building and yet as softly flowing as the balustrades; the whole strikes a "rustique" note in the new idea of nature which Primaticcio and Palissy had introduced.

151

Diana at her bath, Diana metamorphosing Actaeon into a stag, Diana the huntress, Diana goddess of night (day was good enough for the plain Medici features of the Queen)—Diana was hymned in bronze, marble, tapestry, and paint throughout two reigns. The mistress of two kings had, indeed, an archetypal beauty, an ideal perfection of form and face if we can trust the artists who portrayed her. But can we? Did the beauty we see create a model for the School of Fontainebleau, or was it the artists who created an ideal of beauty which *la belle Diane* was forced to live up to? The marble statue of Diana-Diane embracing the stag-François was originally a fountain at Anet, and scholars still debate whether it should be attributed to Goujon, Cellini, the young Pilon, or some unknown genius. As for the painting, it is directly inspired by the cast of a classical statue Primaticcio brought from Rome, but the figure could not be more

Luca Penni (active 1537–56), attributed. Diana Huntress (Portrait of Diane de Poitiers?). c. 1550. Panel, $75^3/_8 \times 52^3/_8''$. The Louvre, Paris.

◀ Jean Goujon, attributed. The Diana of Anet. Before 1554. Marble, height without base 61″. The Louvre, Paris.

unclassical with its thin legs and thighs, swelling belly, high-placed pointed breasts, tiny head—the hallmarks of the International Gothic style transmuted here into the embodiment of Mannerist grace. A goddess indeed—and an experienced huntswoman—her feet scarcely touch the ground, and the slow coil of her satin drapery lends a floating rhythm to the body in its silent gliding, interrupted only by the quizzical look with which Diane measures the invisible interloper. It may be foolhardy even to risk such a suggestion, but to us it seems that no Italian artist of the sixteenth century would paint such a figure, no French artist whose personality is known could. The role of the Netherlanders at Fontainebleau is still only in part explored, and this figure, in both anatomy and the way of painting, has much in common with the style of the men from the North who had studied Italian art either in Italy itself or with the Italians at Fontainebleau.

153

War and jousting apart (it was in a tourney that Henri was accidentally killed), it was a woman's court, and remained so through the unfortunate reigns of Henri's sons. Great court ladies bathed in milk or perfumes, and for economy's sake—wars and diplomatic intrigues were expensive—shared their baths. Here, the Duchesse de Villars's suggestive gesture means only that her sister is pregnant, as we gather also from the nurse preparing a layette in the background. For all the subtle rendering of drapery and the contrast of light and dark, the style harks back to the earliest efforts at Fontainebleau. It is a *fin de siècle* painting, cold, stylized, neurotically meticulous. But it has one odd touch: if we imagine the right hands of the two women overlapping, we recognize the languid droop of the hands in Leonardo's *Mona Lisa*, a detail which was continually imitated as the quintessence of elegance.

Entirely outside the sphere of Fontainebleau was Jean Cousin the Elder. His rich warm style suggests both Leonardo and Dürer, and even Giorgione. Indeed, it is tempting to speculate about the direction French art might have taken with native painters like Cousin and without the all-dominating Italian influence at the court. However, his nude Eve is an almost exact transposition of Cellini's Diana over the gate at Anet. The subject itself is enigmatic, but Panofsky connects it with the triumphal arch Cousin designed for Henri's entry into Paris and proposes that the original idea was *Roma Prima Pandora* (Rome is glimpsed in the back-

School of Fontainebleau. Gabrielle d'Estrées and the Duchesse de Villars in Their Bath. c. 1594. Panel, 37³/₄ × 49¹/₄″. The Louvre, Paris.

Jean Cousin the Elder (active 1526–60/61). Eva Prima Pandora. c. 1550. Panel, 38³/₈ × 59″. The Louvre, Paris.

ground), converted later into this thoroughly Humanist symbol in which the First Mother and the mythological Pandora are equated as bringers of evil into the world.

Henri's public career began with triumphal arches. It ended embalmed in marble in the superbly modeled *gisants* which Pilon sculpted for the tomb designed by Primaticcio.

Germain Pilon (c. 1530–90). *Gisants* of Henri II and Catherine de' Medici from their funeral monument designed by Francesco Primaticcio. 1563–70. Marble, length 68⁷/₈″. Abbey Church of St.-Denis, Paris.

The last years of Henri II's reign had been turbulent. The force of his conviction that heresy and sedition were the same thing made a small sect grow finally into a threat to the throne. The reigns of his three sons were tormented by religious and civil war. Peace came only when Henri of Navarre renounced Protestantism—"*Paris vaut bien une messe*" (Paris is well worth a Mass)—to become the fourth Henri and the first Bourbon king of France. To express in art the spiritual anguish of the age, France would have needed a Michelangelo or, at least, a Pontormo or a Rosso (of the years before vanity and François I had corrupted him into a decorator). Lacking such geniuses—and would they have been allowed to speak out in such tense times?—the truth was masked by a mad round of *fêtes*, by a sophistication which mocked at the simple elegance of François's artists. Only Pilon reacted with the vehemence the times deserved. For the monument for the heart of Henri II he had taken as model an engraving by Marcantonio Raimondi of an incense burner Raphael designed for François I, and the three Theological Virtues are scarcely distinguishable from the three Graces, revealing in every line, in every proportion, the still-dominant influence of Primaticcio. Yet this work of 1560 has a repose so unlike anything done for Fontainebleau that one is tempted to think of it as High Renaissance. During the next ten years Pilon worked on the tomb for Henri II, and we have already seen how subtle his modeling became there. By 1580, in the reign of the neurotic Henri III, a throwback to the worst, not the best, of the Medici (Catherine—significantly—loved him the most of her brood of unhappy children), all signs pointed to doom. Sensitive to a changing world in a measure rarely matched by other artists, Pilon withdrew from the foreign idealism François I had imposed on the country. Thoughtfully, losing nothing of the lessons learned from the outsiders, he returned to the native tradition so long neglected except here and there in some remote province of France. He sculpted a tomb, then, with a marble bas-relief *gisant* as emaciated, as wounded in flesh as any Late Gothic mortuary figure. He followed that with an over-life-size *Virgin of Piety* in painted terra cotta, a pyramid in which drapery shrouds the slender face and hands

with a feeling for the drama of every fold comparable only to the great cathedral statues of three centuries earlier. Finally there was this *Deposition* in which every line speaks with pathos, where even light plays a part in the drama, glancing off or caught in the tangles of drapery of the foreground figures in high relief, making specters of the fine-etched, almost flat-relief figures in the background. True, there is something of Michelangelo here, and the figures and composition owe much to a relief by Baccio Bandinelli (from which Pilon also took his *Virgin of Piety*). But what prevails is a completely native expression realized with all the conviction that a centuries-old tradition gave to a great sculptor.

◄ Germain Pilon. Deposition. c. 1580–85. Bronze relief, 18⁷/₈ × 31⁷/₈″. The Louvre, Paris.

Germain Pilon. Monument for the Heart of Henri II. 1560. Marble, height of figures 59″ (urn reconstructed in 19th century). The Louvre, Paris.

François Clouet (c. 1505–72). Portrait of Charles IX of France. 1569/70. Canvas, $87^3/_8 \times 45^1/_4$". Kunsthistorisches Museum, Vienna.

Antoine Caron (c. 1520–c. 1599). The Emperor ▶ Augustus and the Tiburtine Sibyl. c. 1580. Canvas, $50 \times 66^7/_8$". The Louvre, Paris.

The times were blind, or unfeeling, or indifferent to doom. Court portraiture here, as in Florence or Madrid or Munich, was concerned with the rank, not the person, with the trappings of dignity and not the flesh it clothed: time enough for that when it came to carving the last portrait, the *gisant* in which the king returned to universal nakedness. Only in the younger Clouet's crayon portraits, as in those by Holbein, do we glimpse the fleeting moods that compound into a human personality. In painted likenesses, we are asked to admire no more than the sumptuous attire, the new mode the Spanish and the Farnese generals had introduced (there were many of them about, for Spain was busy with its restless Low Countries). And whatever the style of portraiture owed to Italians like Bronzino, it had a greater debt to Anthonis Mor of Antwerp who dashed from court to court with scarcely time to wash his brushes, and to the other Netherlanders who quietly but insistently were trying to inject a note of their native realism into the fantasy world the Italians had invented for the delectation of the French kings. That fantasy world itself was taking on a new oddity. Everyone in Europe was reading Torquato Tasso's *Gerusalemme Liberata* with its tales of chivalry and magic tinged with a new Christian anguish. The outright Gothicism of that strange

epic was stirring imaginations as the fables of gods could no longer do. If with a wave of the wand wizards could transform the real into the surreal, artists must do the same for the theatrical festivities that were the rage. For the French Humanists, the more esoteric ramifications of astrology often took the place held by mythology a century before in Florence (Catherine, now the Queen Mother, was surrounded by astrologers and soothsayers), and this is hinted at by one of the great designers of *fêtes*, Caron, in this Christian subject of the Sibyl predicting the birth of the Messiah. The strangely balletic figures moving in a fantastic stage setting are occult symbols and heraldic emblems, but they are also cryptic allusions to the political maneuvers threatening the real world which lay outside the wonderland of the court.

Perhaps the greatest influence on architecture all through the last half of the century and well into the next was a man who built few buildings, or at least few that have survived. For thirty-five years Du Cerceau published one book after another of designs for triumphal arches, temples, *hôtels*, châteaux, and every kind of decoration. He not only invented new designs with unflagging—if sometimes unpractical—imagination, but his engravings are in many cases the only information we have about buildings by other architects which time and revolutions have destroyed or grossly altered. What he saw in Rome in his early years must have encouraged him to indulge his anticlassical fancy, since the 1540s were the great years of Mannerist building there. Many of his designs are simply not realizable. Here is his interpretation of the central-plan ideal of the Italian Renaissance: on an artificial square island, linked to the shore (of what?) by four bridges, is a château whose core is nothing less than the Colosseum. Off this jut, symmetrically, four wings, one at each side, each connected by an elevated passageway with a guardhouse-cum-Roman temple at the head of each bridge! A stunning idea, but scarcely a design for living, just as the decoration he devised for certain façades is more than any serious home owner could bear to live with or afford. But a large share of the ornamentation

Jacques Androuet du Cerceau the Elder (c. 1520–c. 1584). Design for a Château, engraving from the *Livre d'Architecture*, Vol. III, 1582, plate xx.

Place des Vosges (formerly Place Royale), Paris. Begun 1605.

we recognize immediately as French, whether on buildings, furniture, or tableware, and of whatever century or style, goes back ultimately to Du Cerceau's engravings with their delight in the imaginative, the profuse, and the *piacere-stupore* of International Mannerism. The man also possessed a downright practical streak. No one before him had made any methodical study of what constituted a proper town house, an *hôtel*, for all classes from the merchant to the noble. In the fifty designs he did for these, he set the pattern for comfortable living which has never been lost in France. And in this he was the link between the past, so flamboyantly initiated by François I in his first châteaux, and the future for which the new king, Henri IV, prudently prepared. By the time the new Bourbon king was ready to leave Paris for a higher sphere, Paris was worth rather more than his proverbial Mass. He transformed a medieval city into the modern one we know, opening up broad squares, building bridges and hospitals and universities. Most typical of his projects is the Place Royale, now the Place des Vosges. It was there that Henri II had died in a tourney, and since Catherine could never bear to occupy again the old palace that stood there, she proposed to turn the square into a residential place. Henri IV followed through on this scheme, built comfortable dwellings for the not-too-wealthy, surrounded the square by arcades to contain shops, and planted greenery so that the citizenry might have a pleasant place for its promenades. From this nucleus grew the fashionable quarter of the Marais, the center of social and cultural life under Louis XIV. A dilapidated ruin in our century, it has recently been restored to some of its former gracious beauty.

Jacques Bellange (active 1594–1638), attributed. The Feast of Herod. Canvas, $37^3/_8 \times 28^3/_4''$. Alte Pinakothek, Munich.

Paradoxically, by the end of the century it was not the Île-de-France but certain provinces and adjoining territories in which art came closer to the international current. So true is this that the picture here has been variously ascribed to Jacques Bellange of Lorraine, to Josse van Winghe of Brussels who worked in Rome and Frankfurt, and to other Flemings. It obviously derives from Parmigianino, through engravings or by way of Primaticcio at Fontaineblèau, and from Federico Barocci, one of the last and most exquisite of the Italian Mannerists. But much in it is related to Northern art, especially to that of Spranger at the court of Rudolph II in Prague, whence his influence was spread everywhere by Goltzius' engravings. Nor is it surprising that many details in Bellange's paintings and etchings can be traced to direct imitation of Dürer and Schongauer, to indirect parallels with Bruegel, Bloemaert, and other Netherlanders. Such an international constellation was, by that time, no longer possible in the School of Paris and Fontainebleau, which was imposing a fatal academicism on what had once been fresh and daring. That environment could not produce innovators such as the Brothers Le Nain of Laon or Jacques Callot and, later, Georges de La Tour—the latter two, like Bellange, from Lorraine, an independent duchy maintaining carefully balanced relations with Paris, Prague, the Saarland, and far-distant Florence and Mantua. It suffices to compare this *Feast of Herod* with the presumably almost contemporary *Sacrifice* (p. 164) by Toussaint Dubreuil, the leader of the so-called Second School of Fontainebleau. Bellange's scene is phantasmagoric, the sharp colors bitingly contrasted, the light hallucinatory, the personages spectral (but how did that fleshy, ruff-collared Lorraine gentleman stray into this Biblical orgy?).

Dubreuil's painting is set in correctly classical architecture, no details are ambiguous, the figures are round and solid, the color and light soft and suffused. Bellange looks backward, but also ahead to the imaginative

Jacques Bellange. The Three Marys at the Tomb. c. 1620. Copperplate engraving, $17^{1}/_{8} \times 11^{3}/_{8}''$.

inventiveness of the Northern Baroque. Dubreuil's style would soon harden into an academicism from which France would be saved only by the Roman experience of Poussin.

Like Caron's, Bellange's was a world of theater, of the *fêtes* and ballets and *mascarades* he prepared for the court. His innumerable costume designs and sketches metamorphose everyone—hunters, cavaliers, Turks, blind hurdy-gurdy players and young drummers, pages and great ladies—into dancers moving restlessly, nervously, never violently, in some infinite ballet in which no human foot rests long on earth. In his etchings on religious themes, Christ carrying the Cross looks up self-consciously to gauge the effect of His tragedy, swanlike women cluster about making brave gestures with their handkerchiefs, the spearmen take elegant stances. And yet there is a mystery in them and a mysticism. The Three Marys at the empty tomb of Christ are the height of fashion in their bouffant gowns, and the angel is almost coy. But space becomes a conundrum as the artist makes us look into the cave from an impossibly high viewpoint. Time is doubled as it had rarely been since the Gothic period for we see the women twice over, entering the cave and confronting the angel; and the incredible figures, tall as praying mantises, are themselves supernatural. Even the exquisiteness of the etching technique removes us from any human sphere. We have seen, with Cambiaso and Zuccari in Italy, with El Greco in Spain, some of the forms that Counter-Reformation piety assumed. This is another; it is elegant, mellifluous even, but none the less devout for being completely personal, refined, subtle, neurotically hypersensitive.

Fontainebleau est mort, vive le Louvre. When the center of the kingdom moved to Paris, Fontainebleau died

Toussaint Dubreuil (1561–1602). A Sacrifice. c. 1602. Canvas, 74³/₄ × 55¹/₈″. The Louvre, Paris.

and, with it, the French Renaissance. Its great artists were no more, dead or returned to Italy. Its halls fell into silence, but its lesson remained: the young Poussin came there before leaving for Italy and said afterward that it was the most fitting place to educate a painter and to stimulate his genius; indeed, what he himself painted before he acquired the new classical example of Rome may well be considered the ultimate achievement of Fontainebleau. In the final years of the century, the leadership was taken by Toussaint Dubreuil, a native Frenchman trained at Fontainebleau; by Martin Fréminet, most of whose adult life was spent in Italy; and by Ambroise Dubois, whose fellow citizens in Antwerp knew him as Bosschaert. From the outset, Fontainebleau had been a way station for the Netherlanders on their travels to and from Italy. The role they played there became ever more important but, intruders from a more real world, it was a role that had no place in the fantastic court ballet of Fontainebleau.

THE LOW COUNTRIES

In the years when Masaccio was painting the *Tribute Money*, Jan van Eyck was at work in Ghent on the polyptych of the *Adoration of the Mystic Lamb*. Two planets one would think could never meet. And yet they did, a century later, when Netherlandish artists traveled to Italy and returned home to forge a new native style whose drama lies precisely in the clash between the alien ideals of the Italian and the Netherlandish Renaissances. Spain assimilated the outsiders, France submitted to their arrogant rule. The Low Countries fought out, in art, a struggle of conscience as dramatic as that which, in life, was tearing men's spirits between Reform and Counter Reform. Yet, even in the Quattrocento, Flemish artists left their mark on Italian art, in the new technique of painting in oils that they invented, in their more frank, more "friendly" relationship with reality: when the triptych Hugo van der Goes had painted for Portinari, the Medici's agent in Bruges, arrived in

z

Ioannes a ductecum Lucas ductecum Fecit.

Hieronymus Cock (c. 1510–70). The Obsequies of Charles V at Brussels, December 29, 1558 (detail). Copperplate engraved by Jean and Lucas van Duatecum, printed by Christophe Plantin, Antwerp, 1559.

Florence around 1480, it gave to Ghirlandaio and others a new feeling for realism. For all that one of the great conquests of the Italians was the depiction of the world about them, it was always in an idealized form. Not a tree, a man, a house, but The Tree, The Man, The House—the Platonic Idea, the essence of what those things should be in their purest forms. The Netherlanders' vision was more microscopic: a blade of grass was a blade of grass in a particular field at a particular time. Man himself was a humble creature, no hero or god, and this was as true of Madonnas as of merchants. Where the Italians understood man through his emotions as expressed in movement and gesture, the Netherlanders defined him by the clothes he wore, the objects he dealt with, the environment in which he lived. For that reason, in Netherlandish painting landscape and interiors assumed the importance Italian painting reserved to the movements of men's bodies. This meant, however, that it was less a question of *what* one painted than of *how*. Light became an essential ingredient, the all-clarifying, all-defining element in which man and nature had their existence (for the Northerners, light was something precious, a token of God's grace; the Italians took their sunlight for granted). Space was defined by light, not by perspective lines, and so there was, at one and the same time, a broader panorama of vision and a more precise account of everything that lay within that panorama. This was in no way an "inferior" or "retarded" approach but, quite simply, the *alternative* approach by which the Northerners created their own Renaissance. All arguments about whether fifteenth-century Flemish art is "Gothic," "Late Gothic," or "Renaissance" must give way before the simple fact that around 1420, at the same time as in Italy, the Flemish brought into being their own new kind of art full of promise for the future, and that too was a rebirth, a renaissance. And that is why Van Eyck's clarity, Van der Weyden's dramatic monumentality, Dirck Bouts's equilibrium, Van der Goes's symbolic realism, Memling's calm poetry, and even Bosch's and Grünewald's visionary jeremiads belong as surely to the Renaissance as does the art of Piero della Francesca, Masaccio, Botticelli, Ghirlandaio, Raphael, and Michelangelo.

Look back at Masaccio's *Tribute Money*. There, light models the figures as if out of clay; they absorb it and it shapes their forms into a three-dimensional, convincing reality. Here, with Rogier, a bolder Northern light sculpts them, carves them out of marble so that it seems as if only a convulsion of the earth could displace them from their gestures of eternal grief. And yet all of them, even the Magdalen contorted in a strange dance of mourning, are intensely human, absorbed in the tragic event. One senses their human character, their human failings. Their faces are not, like those of Masaccio's Apostles, the faces of idealized heroes modeled after Roman portraits. And even more than in their gestures, the drama of the moment is expressed

by the folds of their garments—hard and cracking with the vehemence of the Magdalen's lamentation, soft and flowing for the gentle Saint John, dignified in the brocades of the compassionate burgher who supports Christ's legs. Everything is observed, analyzed, noted—the tender, almost boyish flesh of the Christ is perhaps idealized, but His beard has grown in the long hours of agony. Without landscape, only a sensitively shaded golden box enshrines a composition of curves and countercurves. But the wisps of plants in the foreground can be named, they have been looked at and studied and are not an artist's fancy. This was what Van Eyck had discovered earlier, that art lies as much in the analysis of what already exists as in the Italians' synthesis of the real and the ideal. But such observation of the real was never indiscriminate. A century would pass before artists would attempt a "slice of life." Not man but God created every object, and so a blade of grass or a flickering candle is imbued with meaning, becomes a symbol, becomes more than it is.

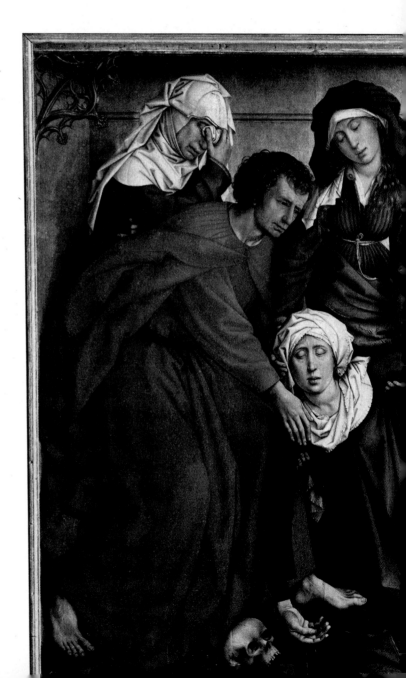

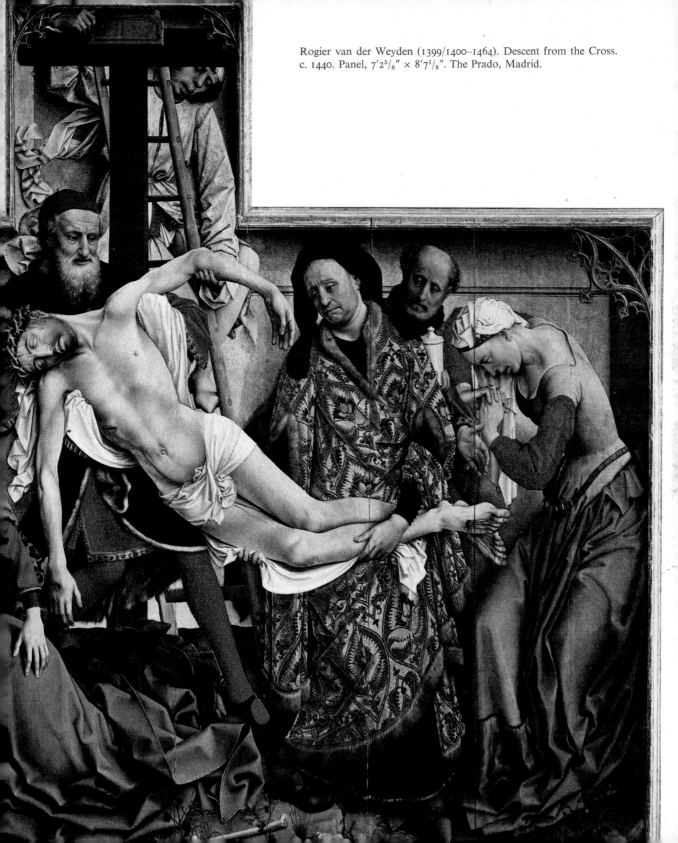

Rogier van der Weyden (1399/1400–1464). Descent from the Cross. c. 1440. Panel, 7'2⅝" × 8'7⅛". The Prado, Madrid.

Jan van Eyck (c. 1390–1441). Giovanni Arnolfini and His Bride Jeanne de Chenany. 1434. Panel, 33 × 22½". National Gallery, London.

Quentin Metsijs (1465/66–1530). ▶ The Money-Changer and His Wife. 1514. Panel, 28 × 26¾". The Louvre, Paris.

In this wedding portrait daily existence is raised to a mystery, both by the perfection of the art which renders it and by the meaning infused into everyday objects. When we have pointed out the significance of the waiting bed as a symbol of conjugal fidelity, of the dog as a symbol of trust, of the single candle burning by daylight as a symbol of Christ, when we have noted that the fully dressed pair have removed their shoes because they stand on the holy ground of matrimony, when we have seen that the mirror reflects two other persons who must be in the room (one of whom is the artist himself, since above it is written *Johannes de eyck fuit hic 1434*), there remains the crystalline light which pours in through the open window to touch and shape and purify everything in the bridal chamber, and is the symbol of God's sanctifying grace. And this light is superbly calculated to unify every form and color in the painting as rigorously as perspective unifies every element in Piero della Francesca's works. Without the four sun-tipped pieces of fruit at the window, the entire delicate structure of the picture might collapse: the humblest object here is a necessary part of the world order, of pictorial order. Not, then, "reality" but rather that transfiguration we call art, the elevation of the visible, the impermanent, into an image of eternity. With a continuity unknown

in Italian art, eighty years later the same moral aesthetic still held. The *Money-Changer and His Wife* is no mere scene of genre. It is a sermon on the vanity of earthly goods. The round mirror is a symbol of human frailty, the scale signifies justice and Last Judgment ("Ye shall do no unrighteousness in judgment, in meteyard, in weight, or in measure. Just balances, just weights" [Leviticus 19:35f.]), and the light makes the woman's face the main subject of the picture: greed seduces her spirit from the pious thoughts of the prayer book lying open before her.

Early Netherlandish painting was largely concentrated in Bruges, the seaport which traded with the world. But Bruges's harbor silted up and its wealth declined at the very time the Low Countries were assuming a major role in the world empire of Charles V. By the early sixteenth century, both commerce and culture had found a new home in Antwerp. There Metsijs came to know Sir Thomas More and Erasmus as well as Dürer, Holbein, and Lucas van Leyden. Lucas, in a sense, opens a new era in Netherlandish art. A boy prodigy as an engraver, with a skill surpassing even Dürer's at that time, his prints quickly reached Italy, where even a Marcantonio Raimondi plagiarized his landscapes as settings for Michelangelo's figures. Lucas himself sought out everything he could learn of art abroad—he outfitted a boat and, with Gossaert as companion, sailed to all ports in the Low Countries where artists could be found. From Gossaert and Barend van Orley, both recently returned from Italy, and from Marcantonio's engravings after Raphael and Michelangelo, he formed his own, perhaps imperfect, idea of the Italian Renaissance. In the *Last Judgment* he exploited his new-found interest in the nude, something scarcely tried before in the Netherlands. He associated his nudes with the familiar demons of the Northern Hell and set them in an infinite space where they rattle about a little like dry bones in a charnel house without achieving the awesome naked grandeur of that high point of the early Italian Renaissance, Signorelli's *Last Judgment* in Orvieto. Lucas' vast empty space is simply a *reductio ad infinitum* of the landscapes created by Van Eyck, Dirck Bouts, Gerard David, and Hieronymus Bosch, in which the precise fact is observed as through a hand lens and placed into a whole which is looked at as if through the wrong end of a telescope. There is something familiar about these landscapes expressive of a hunger for limitless space on the part of men from a country so flat that a hillock suffices as one of nature's monuments: the only other place where landscape developed as a great art was in waterlocked, treeless Venice. They have been called "landscapes of fact." They are, more truly, "landscapes of imagination," and it is this which explains their irresistible romantic appeal, a poetry built out of yearning for the unattainable, not out of quotidian familiarity.

Lucas van Leyden (1494–1533). The Last Judgment. 1526? Center panel 8'9⁷/₈" × 6'7/₈", side panels 8'8¹/₈" × 2'6¹/₈" each. De Lakenhal Museum, Leyden.

Joachim Patinir (c. 1475–1524). Heaven and Hell. Panel, $25^{1}/_{4} \times 40^{1}/_{2}''$. The Prado, Madrid.

Jan Swart van Groeningen (1490/1500–1553/58). Saint John the Baptist Preaching Repentance. 1528–30. Panel, $29^{3}/_{4} \times 44^{3}/_{8}''$. Alte Pinakothek, Munich.

Pieter Bruegel the Elder (1525/30–69). The Hay Harvest (The Month of June). 1565? Panel, $44^7/_8 \times 62^1/_4''$. National Gallery, Prague.

Flemish landscapes are not photographic. They were composed as objectively as Italians posed nude models. Viewing points are always very high, as if the artist gazed down from a cliff, so the horizon is in the upper third of the picture. In the middle ground hills rise to tall crags, in the background mountains with a distant watercourse or seacoast bleach out to palest blue. It is the reality of the facts in such landscapes which makes us believe them. It also makes us believe the outlandish grotesqueries of Bosch and Bruegel, because the world in which they occur *seems* real. We accept Patinir's heretical-Humanist notion of a Christian Heaven and Hell separated not vertically but horizontally by the River Styx, with Charon ferrying a naked Christian soul to a Hell so natural that orange trees and flowering bushes prosper unscorched by the flames of the Fiend (conspicuous by his absence—an innovation in religious art). Swart's Saint John preaches to a strange crew—turbaned Turks, Flemish girls, Biblical ancients, a stovepipe-hatted burgher, and even someone who might be a green-tiaraed pope. But we accept this time-space medley because it *looks* real. Bruegel's disc-faced puppets become human because the rakes they carry, the scythes they hone, the beans they harvest are more realistic than they are. All this is because what we see is neither truly real nor wholly imaginary: it is God's universe infused with symbolism, in which man is a grain of sand, not the measure of all things as Italy thought he was.

Jan van Scorel (1495–1562). Mary Magdalen. 1527–29. Panel, 26³/₈ × 30¹/₈″. Rijksmuseum, Amsterdam.

Jan Gossaert, called ▶ Mabuse (1478/88–1532). Danaë. 1527. Panel, 44³/₄ × 33″. Alte Pinakothek, Munich.

The Low Countries were blind to the seductions of the Italian Renaissance until late in the fifteenth century. In essence, Italian art aimed at the conquest of form, Netherlandish art at individual expression. The first artist to be deeply changed by his "grand tour" was Scorel—it was a tour which took him through Germany where he met Dürer, to Venice, Crete, Cyprus, Jerusalem, and at last to Rome where he became curator of the papal treasures under the Dutch pope Adrian VI. What he returned with was less a vision of Roman Antiquity than a Venetian feeling for the softness of light, for colors in pale, liquid harmonies, for richness of textures. For his part, Gossaert became infatuated with the external trappings of the Renaissance. An intellectual artist in the service of the intellectual Philip of Burgundy (whose Humanist convictions helped him reconcile the contradiction between his post as archbishop and his taste for erotic pictures *à l'antique*), Gossaert brought back his own version of the Quattrocento, the "mineral" world of Antique statuary and of Mantegna (neither Raphael nor Michelangelo was at work in Rome when he was there). He was obsessed with the nude, in a country and at a time when to paint a nude was to fly the banner of rebellion. But there is always something a little uncomfortable about his nudes, a naked scandal in that Northern light; and Netherlandish elements jostle rudely with Italian, as here where a peasant girl is disguised as the mythical Danaë in an exquisite classical loggia looking out on a bizarre mélange of Romanesque, Gothic, and Renaissance buildings such as no city in the world could offer, the dreamworld of an artist caught up in the jumbled memories of far places.

IOANNES · MALBODIVS · PINGEBAT · 1527

Wilhelm Printz zu Vra[...]
Graff von Nassaw
Hätzernalien Vegern[...]

One of the artists who traveled was Mor—to Rome, Lisbon, Madrid, Augsburg, London—recording everywhere the features, and sometimes the character, of the great of the world. From portraits by Van Eyck, Van der Weyden, or Memling we get the quiet, intimate essence of a man, the still center of a private being. Mor's noblemen are public figures, grave, with an almost weary resignation at the burdens of state. International court etiquette was Spanish, aloof with the pride of position, and Mor caught this beautifully, along with the details of international court costume which likewise had become Spanish. Pride was all: princes stand, burghers sit. His portraits were not for the home or family but for great halls lined with the effigies of ancestors as nobly cold as Roman busts. His sitters were all Men of Destiny, like William of Orange who in a few years was fated to lead the Low Countries in revolt against Spain. Group portraits were a special problem, one peculiar to Holland, growing out of the citizens' militias against Spain, and fully solved, artistically, only by Frans Hals and Rembrandt and yet of special appeal to a country which judged men by what they were and did. Here character is foremost: the young dandy swanking it self-consciously in a cream satin doublet, older men in hard-to-hold poses showing off an elegant sword here, an orange sash there—private faces in a public place. Before Ketel such groups were made up of rigid stereotypes. With him there is a real effort at composition achieved through animated gesture. Immobile as are the poses, movement is created by the legs which crisscross like those of walking figures in a slow-motion film. Here there is more than dignity, there is character—the focus on individual men in their own world which was as central to Netherlandish art as was, for Italian art, the study of Man as an ideal being.

◄ Anthonis Mor (c. 1517–76/77). Portrait of William I the Silent of Orange-Nassau. 1555–56. Panel, 41³⁄₈ × 32¹⁄₂″. Staatliche Gemäldegalerie, Kassel.

Cornelis Ketel (1548–1616). The Company of Captain Rosecrans and Lieutenant Pauw. 1588. Canvas, 6′9⁷⁄₈″ × 13′5³⁄₈″ (cut down from the original). Rijksmuseum, Amsterdam.

Netherlandish "realism" was anything but an unsophisticated hymn to the good things of life. Even seventeenth-century Dutch still lifes are more often than not parables of the vanity of earthly goods, and this moralizing tradition was in full sway a century earlier when the clash between new doctrines and old loyalties was being settled by fire and sword. Aertsen is held up as the master realist of domestic life with his kitchen and market scenes. But we know little of his religious pictures because many were smashed by the iconoclasts and, embittered, he turned to painting genre scenes. Yet those are no mere glimpses of daily life. His women in kitchens are almost heroic symbols of domestic virtue, and in the background of his most naturalistic scenes there is almost always a subtle allusion to some well-known Biblical story which makes of them not genre scenes but moralistic sermons. At first glance, this rowdy carousal seems mere genre, and that is what it is commonly considered. Look closer. There are two figures oblivious to all save pleasure—the drunkard bawling a vulgar ditty, the youth intent on a perilous dance over eggs. At the door a child is about to enter, but he has a heroic air and gazes upward, not at the dancer's feet as one might expect. Behind him, his parents remain beyond the half-open door, as if sending the child alone to an appointed task. But the mother with her white hood, her index finger pointing to the child, her gaze modestly lowered—could she be the Madonna? And behind her, the father has exactly the air of concentration Saint Joseph wears in the Holy Families of Raphael and Michelangelo (and—startlingly—he seems copied directly from the portrait of Michelangelo as Heraclitus in Raphael's *School of Athens*!). In the foreground the young girl points to the door warningly, in the background the aged pair—Joachim and Anna?—signal the drinker and dancer to stop. The final touch—beyond the window tiny figures gather fruit: "Whatsoever a man soweth...shall he also reap."

Pieter Aertsen (1508–75). The Dance over the Eggs. 1557. Panel, 33¹/₈ × 50″. Rijksmuseum, Amsterdam.

Pieter Bruegel the Elder. The Blind Leading the Blind. 1568. Canvas, $33^7/_8 \times 60^5/_8''$. Museum of Capodimonte, Naples.

In the Netherlands of His Imperial Majesty Philip II, wise men spoke in parables. Loyalties were divided, false leaders led the populace into traps, foolish ones into disasters. Erasmus had praised Folly, and Bruegel knew why, just as he knew why Sebastian Brant found so many passengers for his Ship of Fools. Bruegel knew his Bible also: "Let them alone: they be blind leaders of the blind. And if the blind lead the blind, both shall fall into the ditch" (Matthew 15:14). Christ had said this of the Pharisees, and in 1568 there were plenty of hidebound conservatives who counseled a caution that could lead only to catastrophe. Hieronymus Bosch had represented this subject before, and Bosch was Bruegel's guide, a guide with eyes wide open on the folly and madness of mankind. Bosch's and Bruegel's creations, however bizarre they may strike us, are never the gratuitous play of a painter's wit. They are sermons in paint on texts drawn from folk proverbs or Biblical passages familiar to their time, if not always to ours. No matter how wild the fancy, we believe them and are moved by them, because their message is universal and also because they are rendered with a lancet-sharp observation of things and people. Bruegel's blind men act out a comic tragedy. Their faces express trust, terror, bewilderment, fatal resignation (we are irresistibly reminded of the horror of men's blind interdependence in a great parable of our own time, Beckett's *Waiting for Godot*). Certainly there are landscapes and scenes of peasant life by Bruegel which seem to be without occult meaning—but the tiny sower in a vast country landscape may be followed by a tinier bird which promptly devours the seed, and at the end of the path where peasants dance may stand a gallows tree.

Pieter Bruegel the Elder. The Return of the Hunters (The Month of February). 1565. Panel, $46^1/_8 \times 63^3/_4''$. Kunsthistorisches Museum, Vienna.

Bruegel spent almost two years in Italy in his mid-twenties. Because he never made a display of Renaissance motifs—garlands, pillars, *putti*, and the like—it is generally said that his Northerner's spirit was indifferent to the southern Renaissance. But what he took from Italy was something more significant than a ragbag of Antique bric-a-brac. He learned, as none of his contemporaries in the Low Countries did, how to create a unity out of the innumerable accurately observed details which make up his pictures, and unity, we have seen, was a fundamental aim of the Italian Renaissance. This winter landscape is a network of diagonals and horizontals which run parallel or intersect sharply. There are no curves; the pattern itself is as rigid as the winter cold. The eye is led inexorably to the leaden sky and icy peaks in the distance with their threat of an even more intense cold. With the fewest possible colors, made even colder by their contrast with the skillfully placed patches of brick red receding into the distance (a technique strangely reminiscent of Chinese ink-and-watercolor landscapes), a complex composition is held together as tightly as the village itself is imprisoned in the grip of winter: composition and meaning are one. Similarly, in the parable of the blind men, the diagonal composition plunges fatally to the disaster ahead; placed on a horizontal, the figures would lose much meaning and drama. As skillfully and as consciously as Leonardo, Titian, or Tintoretto, Bruegel makes a single expressive unity out of color, form, and meaning.

Here is a portrait of a happy Dutch family. Or is it? Why is the infant nude, and so much like a herculean Christ Child drawn by, say, Michelangelo? Why does he play with his mother's rosary and clutch its carved crucifix? Why does the next child hold a cherry so much like a rosary bead? Why are the parents pensive, the children innocently unconcerned? Why is bread the object closest to the infant, and farthest from him the empty wine glass the father holds in almost ritual manner? Were this picture dated a century later, we should know the answer: in Dutch still lifes of the seventeenth century the half-consumed meal is a symbol of the transitoriness of life; in family portraits, a dead member appears among the living, distinguished only by some oddity in dress or pose.

Maerten van Heemskerck (1498–1574). Family Portrait. c. 1532. Panel, 46⁷/₈ × 55¹/₄″. Staatliche Gemäldegalerie, Kassel.

Maerten van Heemskerck. Christ Crowned with Thorns. Panel, 38⅝ × 53½″. Frans Hals Museum, Haarlem.

International Mannerism struck the Low Countries with a vehemence nothing in Italy or in the Low Countries themselves could have led one to expect. It was as if, drunken with the *terribilità* of Michelangelo and with a Northern mingled hate and desire for naked flesh, a latent sadism exploded into consciousness. To Heemskerck, Rome meant Michelangelo's *Last Judgment* and ancient ruins. Returned to Haarlem, his Roman experience became an obsession, a nightmare of shattered columns, nudes with muscles that take on a threatening life of their own. With Cornelisz there is almost an obscenity of violence. The circular composition explodes out to the periphery (as in Raphael's *Expulsion*) but also swoops backward in depth; light glares and is streaked with menacing shadows; one senses an almost repulsive erotic delight in the virtuoso rendering of tortured flesh. All this is made so much the more painful by a hint of the academicism which, within a few years, would make Guido Reni's and Poussin's treatments of the same subject into frozen studies in the repertory of facial expression and body movement. Psychological, even theological, as was this preoccupation with the nude, it had yet another origin: in 1543 Andreas Vesalius of Brussels published his treatise on anatomy, illustrated with skeletons and flesh-stripped bodies in dramatic poses; it had as revolutionary an impact on men's thoughts about their bodies as Copernicus' treatise on astronomy had on their conception of the universe.

Cornelis Cornelisz van Haarlem (1562–1638). Massacre of the Innocents. 1591. Canvas, 8′10¼″ × 8′4³/₈″. Frans Hals Museum, Haarlem.

Joachim Wttewael (1566–1638). The Wedding of Peleus and Thetis. Copper, $6^1/_4 \times 8^1/_4''$. Alte Pinakothek, Munich.

Heemskerck and Cornelisz worked in Haarlem, a Protestant center. To them, Catholic Italy and its Counter-Reformation fervor were profoundly unsettling—despicable, they thought, but at the same time teeming with seductions. Italian art was made for aristocrats; their Dutch clients were burghers who appreciated a hell-fire sermon in paint. For Wttewael and Bloemaert in Catholic Utrecht the assimilation of the alien style was easier, and their contact with Fontainebleau showed them the way to a refined, hypersensitive, aristocratic style. Wttewael seems to have no more compunction about painting a riotous bacchanal of the gods for some wealthy collector of erotica than had Giulio Romano, years before, in his frescoes for a duke's pleasure palace. His virtuosity is so much the more astounding when one thinks of the tiny size of this picture painted on copper. We recognize his nudes from their Italian and French cousins at Fontainebleau; his clouds which so much resemble the fleshier portions of human anatomy come directly from Correggio, his ice-blue distances from Netherlandish landscape painting, his loose-flowing form—a garland of nudes—from International Mannerism which conceived as one of its main tasks the destruction of logical space in favor of an irrational expressiveness. But the most direct debt is to the most sensitive of all the Flemish artists of the time, Bartholomeus Spranger, whom we shall meet again in Germany. From Spranger's lyrical alchemy of forms and colors (known in Utrecht only through the brilliant engravings by Hendrik Goltzius) came Bloemaert also. His *Judith* seems to flow almost formlessly. The main action is dwarfed by the huge foreground figures who point to it but are otherwise uninvolved. The draperies seem crushed paper, the figures themselves melted wax. Torches and flambeaux lead into the picture but end in a nothingness of dark (compare Titian's *Crowning with Thorns*). The forms are torn apart, shredded by flickering light and impenetrable darkness. Space, flesh, story are all fragmented to create that believable unbelievable world which art has always been—and this is the essence of Mannerism, whatever guise it may assume.

Abraham Bloemaert (1564–1651). Judith Shows the Head of Holophernes to the People. 1593. Panel, $13^5/_8 \times 17^1/_2''$. Kunsthistorisches Museum, Vienna.

Bruegel's youngest son, born a year before his father's death, was no peasant painter. Protégé of a great ecclesiastical and secular lord, Cardinal Federico Borromeo, his tastes were refined, his attitude cosmopolitan. Indifferent to his father's parables in paint, subject matter for him was merely the pretext for luscious, velvety painting (whence his name "the Velvet Bruegel"). This *Earthly Paradise* is, in fact, not at all a religious picture: God, Adam, and Eve have no role to play that could not be replaced by a tawny lion and a red-flowering bush. Its true name is merely *Earth*, and it is part of a series of the Four Elements done for the Cardinal. The formal structure of earlier Netherlandish landscapes is abandoned here in favor of a "slice of nature" which appears to be perfectly spontaneous but, like the later landscapes of Claude Lorrain, is carefully framed at either side and has a central focus of interest—a horse and two trees. What matters here is only the lush landscape and the brilliant portrayal of animals. The art of a moralizing father became, with the son, hedonistic, epicurean, Georgic, a delight to the eyes but no challenge to the mind. In fact, the son owed less to his father than he did to Coninxloo who fled from Antwerp to escape religious persecution and, with other

Jan Bruegel the Elder (1568–1625). Allegory of Earth: The Earthly Paradise. 1621. Copper, $18^1/_8 \times 26^3/_8''$. The Louvre, Paris.

Gillis van Coninxloo (1544–1607). Forest Landscape with Heron Hunters. 1605. Copper, $16^1/_2 \times 32^1/_4$″. Historisches Museum der Pfalz, Speyer.

refugees, created a school of landscape art in German Frankenthal. Early in his career Coninxloo used the traditional formula of warm colors in the foreground, various shades of green in the middle ground, icy pale blue in the distance. In this late work, landscape has taken on a life of its own. We are no longer observing from some remote high viewing point. Instead, we enter into the heart of the forest, prisoners in the tangles of a vegetable world. The luxuriating masses of green lie all around us. They do not stop at the picture's edge but go on—before, behind, to the right and left—in a timeless continuum of green. Yet there is form, a new kind of form created by the gaps in the green mass which draw our eye into depth. The fact that there is form —art—makes us accept as completely true this forest where the force of live sap makes trees twist from their naked brown roots to their green tops, where thick-leaved branches swirl in the air, where tiny animals are more at home than the tiny huntsmen who are no more than dispensable intruders. Not by geometrical form but by superbly spaced nuances and harmonies of green does Coninxloo create unity, and that is already an art of the Baroque, not of Mannerism; it is close, too, to that Romantic conception of the nineteenth century in which man loses himself in nature.

We have seen already how much the diffusion of a style owed to engravings and woodcuts. Without them, art everywhere might have remained provincial. With them, artists in Italy learned from Dürer and Lucas van Leyden, artists in Portugal, Paris, or Lorraine, in Antwerp or Munich quickly came to know what Michelangelo had done, or Raphael, or Titian. But engraving was no mere primitive makeshift before the invention of photography. Men like Mantegna, Parmigianino, Pieter Bruegel the Elder, Heemskerck, and Vos either themselves used the burin or supplied the engravers with drawings. Here the engraver's tools lend textural elegance to every detail, from the tiny figures in the summerhouse to the still life in the foreground. Like landscape, still life was becoming an independent art form. The increased wealth in the northern Netherlands meant that humble citizens desired pictures and could afford them. Great princes in the sixteenth century had their "*Wunderkammern*," but ordinary citizens cultivated gardens with the same passion for the beautiful or exotic, and it was natural that they should wish to have "portraits" of their rarer specimens. From the

artist this demanded a technique as meticulous as miniature painting. With Bosschaert each flower is isolated and defined with the same care as if it were a figure in a group portrait, and an even, clear, cool light bathes them all equally. Bosschaert's own hallmark is the placing of the vase on a window ledge with a pale,

◄ Maerten de Vos (1532–1603). Earth, from a series of the Four Elements. Copperplate engraving by Crispijn de Passe the Elder (c. 1565–1637), 8 × 8³/₄".

Ambrosius Bosschaert the Elder (1573–1621). Still Life of Flowers and Shells. c. 1619. Panel, 25¹/₄ × 18¹/₈". The Mauritshuis, The Hague.

contrasting distant view behind it. However, there must be no misunderstanding: flower paintings and other types of still life were no more done from "nature" than, say, a court portrait by Bronzino or Coëllo. The arrangement was studied and deliberate, and flowers blooming at different seasons were often shown together. A fixed hierarchy was always respected—roses at the bottom, tulips in the middle, some superb or very rare flower at the top, as the yellow iris here. Often a tiny fly was introduced to make a formal balance with the artist's signature, and there is an additional symbolic note—one shell comes from the East Indies, the other from the West Indies. Only the details are "naturalistic," never the whole, and this we have seen to be true throughout Netherlandish painting.

Anthonis Mor. Portrait of the Wife of Jehan Le Cocq. 1559. Panel, $33\,^5/_8 \times 23\,^1/_4''$. Staatliche Gemäldegalerie, Kassel.

A middle-class clientele meant not only new subjects—flowers, tables set with food, musical instruments lying side by side, game or fish piled in heaps. It also meant a change in portraiture. The family desired a true likeness, not an idealized emblem of dignity as in court portraiture. The woman pictured here was the wife of Jehan Le Cocq, an obscure Netherlands madrigal composer who may—or may not—have been *maestro di cappella* at the Este's court in Ferrara; and that is her sole claim to fame. She is plebeian, coarse-featured but not unsympathetic, and one senses the embarrassed constraint of a good Flemish wife and mother transplanted into an alien land, a constraint not eased by the fact that Mor, much more at home in court circles, obviously had in mind such chillingly aristocratic portraits as the court beauty by Pontormo which we saw earlier.

The whole notion of "cultural lag"—that some arts lag behind others—is, in general, a fallacy. If a new style answers the aspirations of a people, it will do so in all fields of art. In the Low Countries, however, Gothic architecture and sculpture were so much an expression of the national character that, in a social situation where aristocrats were increasingly impoverished and the bourgeoisie increasingly powerful, those two arts clung to conservative positions for a long time. Not even under the Hapsburgs was there a single dominant center like Fontainebleau or Granada, and the Empire must have felt that its hold on the rebellious provinces was too unsure to warrant lavish new buildings.

For the most part, architects were content to ornament the native Late Gothic style of buildings with motifs borrowed from Italy. At Nijmegen the local brick was used, with stone reserved for the decoration. Across the parapet are medallions with figures in relief, much as at the Certosa of Pavia. The pediments above the windows are an odd adaptation of the classical form, and each frames a high-relief head projecting out from the

Tommaso Vincidor da Bologna (active 1517–36). Inner Court, Breda Castle. 1536–38.

estries being woven there on cartoons by Raphael. Lacking architectural experience, Vincidor designed a medieval castle disguised as a French château which was trying to imitate a Florentine palace. Many of its borrowed features were impractical for a northern climate—an unroofed courtyard, an open and uninhabitable gallery, a surrounding moat which held the damp. The decorative and functional elements are used incorrectly, as if Vincidor were improvising from memories of his homeland: in the court, Ionic half-columns separate windows which lack pediments, the arcades are beneath an unproportioned frieze of disparate triglyphs and metopes. The result was neither an exemplar of the Italian Renaissance nor an expression of the native Renaissance which by then, in painting at least, had had its own idiom for a century and more.

wall like a Gothic gargoyle. Between the windows on the first floor, statues of emperors set up on consoles look for all the world like pieces lined up for a game of chess. Finally, impractical as it may seem in a climate such as Holland's, the entire façade was painted and gilded. But a thoroughgoing change was coming about in the Netherlands. By 1539 Serlio's books on architecture were being translated. Soon the beautifully imaginative designs of Vredeman de Vries and Floris would play the same stimulating role in the Low Countries as Du Cerceau's were playing in France. And at the same time as the Nijmegen town hall, another town hall was going up in Antwerp which would revolutionize Netherlandish and even European style.

The first building to show clear-cut Renaissance features was designed for Hendrik III of Nassau-Breda by an Italian painter who had come from Rome to Brussels in 1519 to supervise work on the set of tap-

Herman van Herengrave (documented 1554–69). Town Hall, Nijmegen. 1554. (Seriously damaged in 1944–45).

Cornelis Floris deVriendt (c. 1514–75). Town Hall, Antwerp. 1561–66.

Lieven de Key (c. 1560–1627). Façade, Town Hall, Leyden. 1597.

The first building in a thoroughly acclimated Mannerist style was the Antwerp town hall, a massive block, fully architectonic in structure and novel in decoration, neither Italian nor French but wholly Netherlandish and of its time. The rusticated stone at the base makes a happy contrast with the delicate crisscross of classical half-columns and mullioned windows on the upper stories. An open gallery at the top runs across the width of the building, and the geometrical simplicity of the entire façade is set off by the more elaborate three-bay frontispiece with its open round-arched loggias (now glassed in), niches with allegorical statues, escutcheons, obelisks, and, above all, its peaked gable. The gable substitutes for the belfry which crowned Gothic public buildings, and here it is a false front with no roof behind it. Perhaps precisely because it was an adaptation of a native form, the ornamental gable had immense success. For it, Floris devised a new abstract decorative motif, fretwork or strapwork which looks like wood cut out with a scroll saw or like interlacing bands of studded leather. Such patterns had already been used around the windows of Peruzzi's Palazzo Massimo alle Colonne in Rome and in the stucco frames by Rosso and Primaticcio at Fontainebleau, but never with such a completely natural delight in craftsmanship for its own sake and in the rich possibilities of exuberant decoration as a foil for the more austere architectural mass. Denied any more spectacular development by the political and religious conflicts of the times, the style was largely perpetuated in the middle-class dwellings which are the gems of so many Dutch and Belgian cities, and it was diffused throughout northern Europe by the pattern books. Its influence is clear in the Leyden town hall. There too a sober façade, not in brick as was customary but in stone, is made more effective by the elaborate decoration of the gables and bulb-tower (the façade masks an existing medieval building). The new note here is the double staircase, an adaptation from Italian villa architecture, and in it there is even a painterly treatment of light and shadow.

The House of the Three Herrings, Deventer. 1575.

This house of a well-to-do merchant has the merits and the failings of an architecture still concerned with reconciling native and foreign elements. The gable has the Italianate elegance of Vredeman de Vries's imaginative designs, and even has the volutes at either side which became so characteristic a feature of Italian church façades. The broad windows make the middle stories a trap for sunlight, but their lack of any real pediment jars with the classical pilasters. The rusticated bands around the pilasters conceal the shaft, and break up the surface ornamentally, but create an effect of squatness. Despite its "modernity," the house still has much in common with the traditional native half-timbered house, which doubtless explains why this type of building was taken up so enthusiastically in the Netherlands and also in Germany where architecture followed the Netherlandish lead.

One of the finest achievements of the Renaissance in all countries was carved wooden furniture for churches and homes. In this the French shone, with their natural feeling for highly decorated surfaces, and French furniture of the time has a splendid profusion of arabesques, *grotteschi*, and fantastic statuettes. Unlike the roughly contemporary choir stalls of Auch in southwestern France with their exuberant (and quite unchurchly) carved decoration, these Netherlandish stalls have a classical sobriety in which Gothic, French, Italian, and even Spanish motifs are happily reconciled.

Jan Terwen (1511–89). Choir Stalls. 1538–41. Carved ▶
wood. Groote Kerk, Dordrecht.

Almost always part of some architectonic structure—tabernacle, choir screen, tomb, fireplace—statuary was slow in achieving an independent existence in the Low Countries. The first sculptor of international culture was Meit, and his career was, appropriately, international, not local. Born in Worms in Germany, he worked at Wittenberg, at the court of the Regent Margaret of Austria in Malines, at Brou and Besançon, and at Antwerp. His co-workers were often Italian or French, but his development out of a Gothic style into the Renaissance was his own personal discovery. Though he carved nudes, made *putti* and superbly lifelike figures for the tomb in Brou, and finally arrived at something close to Sansovino's style in the *Pietà* at Besançon, there is an honest, openhearted spontaneity in his work which stamps him as very much a man of the North. This is evident in his statuette of Judith. It is odd enough to present the chaste Hebrew widow in the nude, but the body is almost doll-like, indifferent to Italian canons of classical proportions and aiming, rather, at a true depiction of a matronly figure. Further, the alabaster is tinted somewhat naïvely—red lips, blue eyes, darker hair. Meit did, however, break effectively with the national tradition which, in sculpture particularly, restricted the nude to a moral admonition.

Conrat Meit (c. 1475–1550/51). Judith with the Head of Holophernes. c. 1530. White alabaster with painted details, height 11⁵/₈". Bayerisches Nationalmuseum, Munich.

Mone's career was even more international, his art more cosmopolitan. Born in the independent ecclesiastical city of Metz, he worked in Aix-en-Provence and Barcelona, at the courts of Malines and Brussels (in the personal service of Charles V), and throughout the Netherlands. He was directly influenced by Bartolomé Ordóñez with whom he worked on the choir screen in Barcelona and perhaps also in Naples. Subjected to such diverse influences, he seems to have found his Italianate style almost by instinct, although in many ways it is that of the Quattrocento as reinterpreted by Spanish sculptors, and has a strong leaning to the expressive forms of a Bregno or Sansovino. This tomb is remarkable for its invention of a plan quite opposite to the Lombard-French type. On a bier of black marble with alabaster reliefs lies the noble pair classically draped. Four heroes of Antiquity—Julius Caesar, Atilius Regulus, Hannibal, and Philip of Macedonia—replace the customary medieval *pleurants* still used on French tombs. They bear aloft a second bier, and on this, instead of figures in prayer, there is the empty armor of the dead warrior-prince. The effect seems starkly Gothic but is truly Renaissance in its association of a dead ruler with the great men of Antiquity.

Jehan Mone (active 1516–48/49), attributed. Funeral Monument of Engelbert II of Nassau-Breda and His Wife Cimburga of Baden. 1530. Alabaster and black marble. Groote Kerk, Breda.

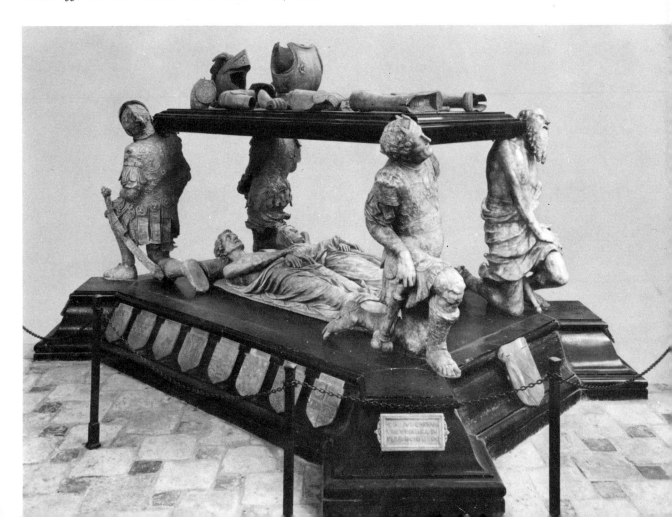

Hendrik de Keyser (1565 –1621). Freedom and Justice, statues on the tomb of William I the Silent, Count of Orange-Nassau. 1614–21. Blackened copper bronze. Nieuwe Kerk, Delft.

By the end of the century Netherlandish sculpture had joined the mainstream of International Mannerism. These tomb statues belong to a set of four extolling the virtues of the dead prince whose portrait by Mor we saw earlier. Their allegorical attributes are taken directly from Cesare Ripa's *Iconologia* of 1593, a compendium of symbols of Antique and Humanist origin which artists had been using for the two centuries of the Renaissance; Ripa's book would be the "artist's bible" for all of the Baroque.

Cornelis Floris de Vriendt. Tomb of Christian III of Denmark. 1568–75. Alabaster, black marble, red marble inlay. Cathedral, Roskilde, Denmark.

The activity of Cornelis Floris was not limited to architecture such as the Antwerp town hall and to publishing pattern books of ornamental designs which diffused his style across northern Europe. He was a sculptor also, profoundly influenced by his sojourn in Italy where, together with his brother, the painter Frans, he attended the unveiling of Michelangelo's *Last Judgment* at Christmas in 1541. His thoroughly Mannerist vein of fantasy is best seen in the fifty-two-feet-high stone tabernacle he made for the country town of Zoutleeuw in present-day Belgium. Its slender tower form is Gothic, but its tiers are organized with an Italian sense of proportion, and the hundreds of small figures, some isolated, some grouped in Biblical scenes, belong to the Renaissance. This tomb was his last work, left unfinished at his death. For King Christian III of Denmark (Roskilde was the old capital) he imitated the royal tombs of France but placed a bodyguard of armed warriors at the four corners, garbed the *gisant* as an Antique warrior with arms and armor, added *putti* and even birds to soften the military note, and constructed a massive base and cornice with richly carved arabesques in relief. In the Low Countries as elsewhere, taste was turning, by the time of his death, to a new classicizing sobriety alien to the flickering play of imagination that had made Mannerism irresistible to both the North and Italy.

Hans van Steenwinkel the Elder (1545–1601), Laurens van Steenwinkel (1585–after 1620), Hans van Steenwinkel the Younger (1587–1630), and Caspar Bogaert (d. 1612). Frederiksborg Castle, near Hillerod, Denmark. Designed c. 1600, built 1602–25.

One of the last and most perfect realizations of the Netherlandish style was the castle of Frederiksborg in Denmark. Stretching over three islands linked by bridges, it has the charm of Du Cerceau's imaginary French châteaux, the massiveness of an Italian palace, the inventive ornamentation of a Dutch or Flemish town hall. In rose brick with creamy sandstone decoration, its neat freshness is as perfectly in tune with nature as Palladio's country villas. The Renaissance came late to Scandinavia but profited from the long experience of the Netherlands. The elder Steenwinkel who designed this castle had lived and worked for many years in northern Germany, then together with Antonis van Opbergen, builder of the Danzig arsenal, emigrated to Denmark where his sons were born; in many ways this is already a native expression, and one of the sons later carried the style to Sweden. For almost a century, religious strife at home and ever-increasing opportunities abroad had helped to disseminate the Netherlandish style to Germany, Scandinavia, France, England, and even to Poland and Bohemia. The designs of Vredeman de Vries—the quintessence of Mannerism—reached everywhere through his voyages and publications, and so did those of Cornelis Floris. A sculptor like Adriaen de Vries, trained in Italy, was called to work in places as remote as Prague, Augsburg, and Frederiksborg. Bartholomeus Spranger painted at Fontainebleau, Parma, Rome, Caprarola, Vienna, and Prague. Anthonis Mor went everywhere a portrait artist was needed, from Lisbon to Vienna to London, and after him there was Frans Pourbus the Younger to portray the aristocrats of Brussels, Mantua, Turin, and Paris. In Spain, Pieter de Kempeneer became Pedro de Campaña and there was also Juan de Flandes; in Italy, Pieter de Witte became Pietro Candido, and no one thinks of Jean Boulogne from Flemish Douai except as Giambologna—without those four artists, neither Spanish nor Italian Mannerism would have been what they were. At Bologna Dionysius Calvaert of Antwerp taught Guido Reni, Albani, and Domenichino, and was an inspiration for the Carracci. Giovanni Stradano—Jan van der Straet of Bruges—was court painter for the later Medici and worked on Francesco I's *studiolo*. The roster of Netherlanders at Fontainebleau was as long as that of the Italians, longer than that of the French. But the fructifying influence of the Low Countries goes further back and runs deeper than these exponents of International Mannerism. The technique of painting with oils was surely their invention, and it became known in Italy before the Quattrocento had ended. We have seen the impact on Italian art of Hugo van der Goes's dramatic realism. Landscape as an independent subject came from the Netherlands. So did still life and genre pictures of everyday activities. Great as were the achievement and influence of the Italian Renaissance, they were matched by those of the Low Countries.

Neck Chain of the Order of the Garter conferred on King Frederick II of Denmark by Queen Elizabeth I of England. 1582. Gold and enameled gold, length 21⅝". The Chronological Museum of the Danish Kings, Rosenborg Castle, Denmark.

In Germany the change from Gothic to Renaissance involved a hundred years of conflict. An old tradition which continued to have a living value held out against a new art which corresponded to the cultural aspirations of no more than a small segment of a population already divided by political and religious controversy. German Gothic sculpture had attained a greatness comparable to that of early Netherlandish painting. It was the expression of a deep piety which saw in the pagan gods of the Italian Humanists not embodiments of man's greatness but only ungodly, malignant trolls and kobolds out of the native folklore. For the first German Humanists, the reawakening of Antiquity did not mean the substitution of new values for old but, instead, a widening of man's intellectual domain to include the language and literature of the past. When the religious conflict broke out, men like Melanchthon and Ulrich von Hutten sought moral guidance not from the Ancients but from within themselves: the divisions ran too deep—the Catholic South against the Protestant North, patricians against plebeians, free cities against the countryside, and at last brother against brother. Maximilian I was the first great seigneur of the new Hapsburg empire, but it was the Hapsburgs' possessions, not their imperial office, which gave them prestige. Maximilian was powerless to impose unity upon an empire in which petty self-interests were defended as violently as great principles. But he saw himself as the heir of the Caesars, and his Humanist aspirations were expressed in his own literary works, odd mixtures of medieval epic forms with a new consciousness of the worth of the individual man. He did not turn to foreign artists but, instead, encouraged such centers as Nuremberg and Augsburg where the transition from Gothic to Renaissance was taking place most painlessly, where artists first saw how to adapt to a new style the purely formal solutions Gothic sculpture had already devised. Thus, this portrait mask—it is hollow behind—by Jörg Muscat of Augsburg is rigidly stylized like Late Gothic sculpture but has something of the new naturalism. Yet it remains a cross between a medieval reliquary head and the expressionistic portrait busts of the late Roman Empire. For his great project, his own tomb, Maximilian called in artists from Munich, Innsbruck, Landshut, Augsburg, and, especially, Nuremberg whose Peter Vischer worked on designs by Dürer. The tomb was intended to be a kind of manifesto: new artists, the new style, a new conception of the sovereign as both an individual in his own right and heir to a great tradition. Around the tomb, enclosed by a grill, Maximilian's ancestors line up like chessmen or—better—like armored automata waiting for clockwork to set them into motion so that, in stately movement, they may adore their descendant who, himself, kneels in prayer in solitary majesty on an upraised dais. Knights and emperors from the old epics of chivalry, legendary wives who brought land and power as dowry, and plain, hard-hitting, tough ancestors, all in sumptuous robes or armorial shells—hard, solid-as-gold values for the Hapsburg dynastic propaganda, they await their orders, not consumed with grief as were the Burgundian and French *pleurants* but swelling with pride at the glory of their scion. Feudal nobles, they are medieval in their shut-off, silent majesty, but already there is something of the Renaissance in their noble stance and magnificent attire.

◄ Jörg Muscat (c. 1450–c. 1527). Portrait Bust of Emperor Maximilian I. c. 1509. Bronze, height 13³/₈″. Kunsthistorisches Museum, Vienna.

Peter Vischer the Elder (c. 1460–1529) after a design by Albrecht Dürer (1471–1528). King Theodoric, from the funeral monument of Maximilian I. 1513. Bronze, height 78″. Court Church, Innsbruck.

Albrecht Dürer. Wehlsch Pirg (Landscape in Southern Tyrol). c. 1495. Watercolor and gouache, $8^1/_4 \times 12^3/_8''$. Ashmolean Museum, Oxford.

Albrecht Dürer. Self-Portrait at Twenty-Nine. 1500. ▶ Panel, $26^3/_8 \times 19^1/_4''$. Alte Pinakothek, Munich.

No one ever made a more decisive break with the past than Dürer. For Masaccio that break was easier: he had only to find the new forms for new conceptions already being bruited about. But Dürer's was a different world, burdened by a still-viable tradition which satisfied the needs of his countrymen; the youth of twenty-four who stopped on his Italian journey to paint this landscape must already have understood what set him apart from his contemporaries. The fact that the mountain scene itself is not very assuming, not really "pictorial," gives us the clue. The young man had accepted the charge of painting what he saw, without regard for formulas, with no man-made rules interposed between his painter's eye and nature. Five years later, in the third of several self-portraits, he could see himself with the same passionate objectivity. It is no accident that here Dürer makes himself resemble Christ, even to the traditional parting of the long locks in the center and the solemn gesture of the hand. The German Renaissance is all here already: in Italy it explored man within a world of men, in the Netherlands it looked long and hard at the world itself, in Germany, from the outset, the chief study of mankind was man himself, and this was what the young Dürer learned from the great heritage of German Gothic sculpture.

Albrecht Dürer. The Madonna of the Rose Garlands. 1506. Panel, $63^3/_4 \times 76^1/_2''$, very much repainted. National Gallery, Prague.

Albrecht Dürer. The Four Apostles. 1526. Panels, $84^7/_8 \times 29^7/_8''$ and $84^1/_2 \times 29^7/_8''$. Alte Pinakothek, Munich.

Space, depth, composition, color, the modeled figure—these were the objective lessons Dürer could take home from Bellini and Mantegna in Venice. No work that he did before his first trip blends all of its components as superbly as does this *Madonna* he painted there. Its composition is still overcrowded and over-decorative, as would be all of Dürer's pictures using many figures, and this reflects the Gothic *horror vacui*. But in his last years he made an extraordinary synthesis of the native tradition and the example of Italy. Through constant purification of means and concepts, in the *Four Apostles* he achieved the monumental simplicity of Masaccio, in which all that counts is man himself. But this too is German and Gothic—not the tortured, formalized complexity of Dürer's immediate predecessors, but the serene nobility and massive dignity of ther thiteenth-century statues of the cathedrals at Naumburg and Bamberg.

Albrecht Dürer. The Last Supper. 1523. Woodcut, $8^3/_8 \times 11^7/_8''$.

Albrecht Dürer. Adam and Eve. 1504. Copperplate engraving, $9^3/_4 \times 7^1/_2''$.

Acclaimed throughout Europe (in Spain he was ranked with Raphael and Michelangelo), admired by his fellow artists, and trusted by both Protestant and Catholic statesmen and Humanists, Dürer none the less had made a lonely choice, and as a painter he created no school and had few followers. It was only as an engraver that his influence reached wherever artists were struggling to find new forms for new conceptions. Nothing was beyond his skill and imagination—saints and Madonnas, peasants, the horrors of the Apocalypse, allegories both Humanist and religious, landscapes—and what was too subtle, too fleeting for the engraver's tools he caught in drawings with pen or silverpoint or charcoal. Whether in woodcuts, in which he tended to a more Gothic expression, or in copperplate engravings which embraced the notions of the Renaissance, it was his extraordinary rendering of the textures of real things which finally made of his prints something more than a means of conveying information. In the *Adam and Eve* the forest is as alive as our Ancestors who truly are Apollo and Venus, even including the classical canon of proportions. But there is a psychological subtlety in the way they act out the archetypal sin which could only come from the artist's long meditation on the Word of God. We know from his writings what value he accorded to imitation of both Antiquity and Nature, and these figures are the ideal synthesis of both those fountainheads. By contrast, Wydyz' boxwood Adam and Eve are a village boy and girl without their clothes. The long-torsoed figures are nuggety, hard, sinewy, though polished smooth and berry-colored. Adam's hair is still in the Riemenschneider Gothic tight curls, he reacts to temptation with naïve emotion, while Eve is little more than a half-smiling doll. Just as Dürer's religious engravings were meant for private meditations, so too in sculpture at that time such small figures began to be made for altars in homes and family chapels where they could be seen close up, for the believer's self-examination of conscience in the silent dialogue between man and God which was soon to blaze forth in civil and national wars. The importance of such beautifully carved tiny statues is both aesthetic and spiritual: they were an exquisite and touching substitute for the great Gothic statues which represented an old form of both art and religion.

Hans Wydyz the Elder (documented 1497–1510). The Temptation. c. 1510. Boxwood, height 6¼". Historisches Museum, Basel.

Not all of Dürer's lessons were lost, not in Nuremberg at least. Both Peter Vischer the Younger and Peter Flötner learned the ways of Italy but sought their own expression for the Humanist notions which were rife in their city. Vischer's *Orpheus and Eurydice* already speaks the language of the Renaissance with fluency, and not only in the Latin Humanist letters of its inscription. The two nudes are placed in a setting which is no more than a lyrical suggestion, yet it suffices—a few flamelike grasses, a trail of sprouting turf. The legend is caught at its most poignant moment (and this too is an art of the Renaissance, as we have seen with Leonardo), the instant at which Orpheus turns to face Eurydice who seems like some Antique figure of unstable Fortune and who now will vanish.

In its concentration of simplicity, in its subtle, absorbed sensitivity, this tiny plaque has a kind of rapt attention to the new world of Renaissance Humanism which could only come from an artist whose native tradition was alien to such a newborn age of innocence. The *Apollo* of Flötner is imitated from an engraving by Jacopo de' Barbari who was in the service of Maximilian, and it is surprising to discover that, compared with the slender grace of the German's statue, the Venetian's engraving is coarse, the figure chunky, the movement unconvincing, the body weight poorly distributed, the anatomy pitiable. Flötner's statue has a light dancing grace, a softness of movement which, it is true, may come from a certain unfamiliarity with the nude but which is also typical of the poetic sensibility of the Nuremberg bronze sculptors in his time. Perhaps if the world had been less unsettled, the ancient gods and goddesses might have made a place for themselves in

Peter Vischer the Younger (1487–1528). Orpheus and Eurydice. 1515/20. Bronze relief, 7 × 5¹/₄″. Museum für Kunst und Gewerbe, Hamburg.

Nuremberg, but the path the Germans took to their Renaissance could not—or, at any rate, did not—lie that way. Dürer might struggle with his theoretical studies of proportions and objective measurements as if Raphael and the Italians had never existed, but German art was to be an art of feeling, not of science. For all of Dürer's preoccupation with nature and the natural, nothing—least of all man—is ever out of place in his landscapes: it is as if God-the-Artist had placed hills and trees in an eternally perfect composition. By Dürer's last years a generation of artists had come up for whom nature and men's souls were caught in the same turmoil of passion, for whom art was a means of expression in our modern sense. This so-called Danube School held sway in an area extending from Regensburg in Bavaria to Vienna, from Salzburg to Innsbruck—a wild Alpine land still, at that time, covered with primeval forests.

Peter Flötner (c. 1490/95–1546). The Apollo Fountain. 1532. Bronze, height 39⅜″, without pedestal. The Peller House, Nuremberg.

Ludwig Refinger (1510/15–49). The Sacrifice of Marcus Curtius. 1540. Panel, 64 × 48/³⁄₄″. Alte Pinakothek, Munich.

Albrecht Altdorfer (c. 1480– ▶ 1538). The Battle of Issus. 1529. Panel, 62¹⁄₄ × 47¹⁄₂″. Alte Pinakothek, Munich.

These two pictures belong to a series done for the Munich Residence of Duke Wilhelm IV of Bavaria. Given the temper of the age, it is not surprising that the battle pictures are thinly disguised references to contemporary events. The *Battle of Issus* portrays not only the defeat of Darius by Alexander the Great but also the victory of Charles V over François I at Pavia. Less obvious is just what individual act of heroism is symbolized by the self-sacrifice of Marcus Curtius who, to placate the gods, rode fully armed into the chasm opened up in front of the Forum by an earthquake. Refinger did not belong to the Danube School. A court painter, he was surely influenced by Mantegna's *Triumphs of Caesar* on his visit to Mantua in the company of Duke Ludwig X. Nevertheless, his view of Rome is as subjective as the Danube School's rendering of nature: a pallid city with an odd brew of architecture piled up into a labyrinthine background through which streams the crowd in a steadily expanding S-curve. The bleached light and sharp pure colors are those of a legendary Rome, all bright and clean and ideal as the Humanists were reconstructing it from the old texts. For all the agitation of the scene, it is controlled, calm, frozen. Not so Altdorfer's battle picture. Man and nature are caught up together in a cosmic apocalypse. Huge plumes vibrate in the clash, myriad lances swirl in ever-diminishing repeated S-curves and figure eights which sweep through city, Alps, islands, crags, and back to the blazing sun from which new S-curves of clouds stream out as if to envelop the holocaust of a world "where ignorant armies clash by night." In panic, Darius flees from dawn to night: his sun has set.

Albrecht Altdorfer. Danube Landscape with Wörth Castle. c. 1520/25. Parchment on panel, 12 × 8³/₄″. Alte Pinakothek, Munich.

The Danube School began at the start of the century with the voyage into Austria of two young painters, Jörg Preu and Lucas Cranach the Elder. To them the primeval landscape revealed new pictorial possibilities Gothic art had never suspected, though Cranach later defected to a quite different style. For all the Danube painters, nature was a kind of sacramental mystery before which man was reduced to humility. To a Giovanni Bellini, nature was a clement atmosphere to be caressed by the eye, a source of peace and delight. For the Germans, it was awesome, imbued with *Sturm und Drang*, with a storm and stress which threaten man (in Cranach's early landscapes fires break out mysteriously and menacingly in the hills). With Coninxloo we feel as if we had entered into a landscape. Here we are engulfed by it, and its secrets are not for us to penetrate. Nature is limitless for Altdorfer, probably the first man to paint a landscape in and for itself, without human figures (Dürer's *Wehlsch Pirg* was only a sketch, not a finished picture). The great castle shrinks to a doll's house in the vastness of sky, lake, mountains, and forest. The sun is setting, the air is still, the valley empty. An inexplicable, suspenseful stillness reigns. Where man made a castle or a road for himself, the tall grass and trees will soon cover it over again. Italian landscape was an ideal setting for man; Netherlandish landscape was something real that was born out of the imagi-

Wolf Huber (c. 1480/85–1553). Agony in the Garden. c. 1530. Left wing of an altarpiece, panel, $23^3/_4 \times 26^1/_2''$. Alte Pinakothek, Munich.

nation; for the Germans it was a pantheistic All, full of symbolism and emotion. With Wolf Huber it became a place of agony. As in his drawings, in which a few calligraphic lines suffice to create a rugged space where moss and mistletoe drip down like tears, here nature itself is stark and cruel. Knife-sharp rocks make a prayer stool for the suffering Christ, the calm pastoral evening light on the hill makes human agony so much the more acute. The sleeping Apostles writhe in a dance of unquiet stupor, Christ's captors within their circle of ashy pale light approach timorously, silently. This is a new way of painting, rich in color, as meticulous in details as manuscript illumination, but broadly sketched with paint that flickers. It is not an art of reality nor, for all its passionate strangeness, is it "Gothic." It is as much an art of the Renaissance, of a new way of seeing and feeling, as that of Grünewald—expressionistic, mystical, laden with profound meaning and deep seriousness.

When Italian influence finally made itself felt directly, Germany was drawn into the orbit of the High Renaissance. As a result of this, its own national character in art was weakened. Responsible, in large measure, was the new emperor, Charles V, whose horizon was supranational, not national as had been Maximilian's. To Augsburg he brought his favorite painter, Titian, and Augsburg was the home of the Fuggers, the great dynasty of merchants on whose ready wealth much of Charles's power rested, and whose agents, like those of the Medici before them, sent home not only news of scandals, intrigues, and political conniving but also the finest works of art from wherever they were. Rich tonality, mellow color, and a feeling for space stamp the Augsburg artist Amberger's portrait as a true product of the Renaissance. It owes much to Italy, but the relaxed, warmly human feeling with which the young Fugger is portrayed has little of Italian formality. And, unlike portraits by Mor or Coëllo, here one feels the personality of the artist himself—warm, intelligent, sympathetic. Beham, on the other hand, came from Dürer's circle in Nuremberg. His over-all tonality is Dürer's, with rich dark colors relieved by areas of white and yellow; but compared with Dürer's portraits there is more space around the figure, more roundness and solidity, at the same time as there is a loss of personality and intensity. It is the work of a fine craftsman for whom what counted in the end was only the pleasure of practicing his art. Barthel, his brother Sebald, and their Italianizing friend Georg Pencz were repeatedly expelled from Nuremberg as "atheists and anarchists" (they spent their exiles working happily as court painters for princes and cardinals).

In Augsburg the family chapel built by the Fuggers in 1509 pointed the way. Inspired by Hans Daucher's freestanding marble *Pietà* on its altar, Hering went a step farther: his *Saint Willibald* is not an altarpiece but an independent, massive monument set in a Renaissance niche. Its rich surface, with calligraphic patterns incised into soft stone, is still quite Gothic. Yet, as in the elder Holbein's painting also, the surface has no Gothic agitation and is almost smoothly buttery. With Holbein, there is no tension in form, composition, or color; even space is an artifact, neither convincing in its depth nor disturbing in its shallowness. Thus, to oppose the Gothic, Augsburg chose Italian classical serenity rather than the native expressionism. The latter, however,

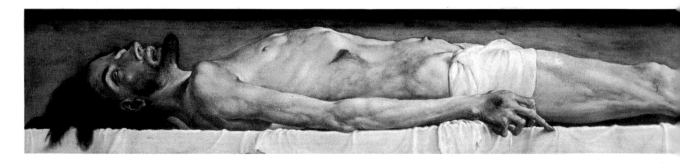

the younger Holbein caught at least once. His *Dead Christ* is a work which, in its detached, cool observation, stands apart from the art of its time. It does not insist on the pathos of the subject but embodies that pathos in the image itself. Dürer might have treated the subject as a scientific study in anatomy, Grünewald as a sermon on the corruption of the flesh as contrasted with the perfection of the spirit. Holbein simply shows us a dead man, the wounds clean, the body still warm with blood, in the hours before it was washed, anointed, wrapped in the shroud, and laid away, before immortality transfigured Jesus into the Christ. It is an image which invites men to meditate on their worldly and spiritual destiny, and as such is far more moving than

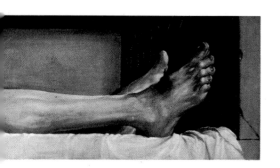

Richier's theatrically exultant skeleton we saw earlier. It is, in fact, the fullest expression which art has ever achieved of a central tenet of Protestantism, a pictorial embodiment of the new thoughts of the German Humanists, that men must live their daily existence in intimate familiarity with both the Son of Man and the Son of God.

Lucas Cranach the Elder (1472–1553). The Three Electors of Saxony: Friedrich the Wise, Johann the Constant, Johann Friedrich the Magnanimous. c. 1535. Central panel 26⁵/₈ × 26³/₈″, side panels 27 × 12³/₄″ each; inscriptions composed by Martin Luther. Kunsthalle, Hamburg.

Holbein, however, never committed himself fully to the new doctrine. Basel, where he had settled early, was torn between the two camps. The Catholic hierarchy had other concerns than decorating churches, the partisans of Reform were opposed to sacred images. Erasmus wrote from Basel, "Here art is dying." Holbein illustrated the Luther Bible, did series of woodcuts for a *Dance of Death* and an *Alphabet of Death*, and painted three fine portraits of Erasmus, but little else. By 1526 there had been riots and repressions, and armed with letters from Erasmus to Sir Thomas More, the artist left for England where, after one brief visit home, he settled as court painter to Henry VIII. Thenceforth the artist of the *Dead Christ* devoted himself to designing decorations and to painting some of the finest portraits the world knows. His premature death by plague cut short a career that, in one sense, had already been cut short by the religious strife. The story can be repeated in infinite variations for other artists in strife-torn Germany and the Low Countries. The crippling effects of the religious conflict were more durable in the North than the panicky exodus of artists from Rome after the sack of 1527. The dearth of commissions for religious art and the constant fear that the iconoclasts would destroy all sacred images diverted prematurely the course of German art into other, less challenging channels. Cranach's career was less agitated, but even more deeply affected by the Reformation. His first works were in the expressionistic style that came to identify the Danube School. Suddenly in 1504 he ceased to be a "tragic" painter. A new repose and formal control entered into his style, something almost Italianate. Soon thereafter he began his "second career," as court painter to the Electors of Saxony. Their capital, Wittenberg, was the seat of a university, the gathering place of Humanists, a headquarters for Luther and Melanchthon, and, soon, the fountainhead of the Reformation. There Cranach became a kind of human factory of art—sixty portraits of his patrons in one year! Plus countless other portraits, designs for court costumes and festivities, religious paintings in which he tried to create a new iconography for the

Reformation, series of woodcuts and engravings with no other pretension than to be violent anti-Roman propaganda, and innumerable pictures on mythological subjects which were either thinly veiled satire or unabashed pretexts for painting nude women. A trip to the Low Countries to portray the eight-year-old future Charles V acquainted him with the Netherlandish and Italian styles and brought a new precision, a grasp of perspective, a greater simplicity to his hearty but somewhat coarse art. The satirist of the Pope knew how to mock at court manners as well. Love makes fools of men—this is the theme of the picture in which, for love of Omphale, Hercules allows himself to be dressed as a woman and learns to spin. The moral is plainly put by the inscription and the two dead partridges, symbols of lust. But the personages are in Wittenberg court costume, and the Hercules, at least, looks like a portrait, perhaps of some courtier at whom the painter himself, or his patrons, wished to poke fun. The urbane if coarse wit, the enamel-smooth meticulousness of the painting are both a long way from the tragic vehemence, agitated brushwork, intense greens, and supernatural fires of his early paintings done in the years just before a great storm broke over Germany and drove a passionate artist into the snug harbor of a progressive but none the less snobbish court.

Lucas Cranach the Elder. Hercules and Omphale. 1537. Panel, $32^1/_2 \times 47^1/_4''$. Herzog Anton Ulrich Museum, Brunswick.

Willing to adapt to changing times, Cranach became the wealthiest burgher in Wittenberg, received more commissions than he could fulfill, and was head of an indefatigable workshop in which his son, Lucas the Younger, learned to paint exactly like his father, though perhaps with a somewhat more flaccid elegance and a paler, rather bleached-out tone. The son became perhaps too much the settled burgher—his Venuses lack the slightly zany air of his father's, and one misses the cryptic smile of a knowing and unashamed cupidity which makes his father's angular nudes a sheer and wicked delight, however much their author may have pretended that they were meant as moral warnings. With Hans Baldung Grien the church tradition died, to be replaced by an authentic strain of moralistic allegory which had its roots in Gothic piety. The figure of Death in all his rotting corruption had been made familiar through Holbein's woodcuts, and now he came to haunt every age of mankind. Protestant morality made of woman a symbol of sin. So she must be shown how Time lies in wait to rob Vanity of her charms (an old medieval theme expressed superbly by François Villon in France); how age will make her withered as her mother (Villon's "The breasts, alack! all fallen in; The flanks too, like the breasts, grown thin"); how Death will find her in a landscape of ancient brown trees and dripping dried ferns. We know the landscape from the Danube School, and it was Baldung's achievement to make that tragic view of nature an element in a moralizing art which was Gothic in its pathos, modern in its conception.

Lucas Cranach the Younger (1515–1586). Venus and Amor. c. 1540. Panel, 66$^1/_2$ × 35″. Alte Pinakothek, Munich.

Hans Baldung Grien (1484/85–1545). Death and the ▶ Three Ages of Woman: Allegory of the Vanity of Earthly Life. c. 1510. Panel, 15$^3/_4$ × 12$^3/_4$″. Kunsthistorisches Museum, Vienna.

Master of the House-Mark. Va-
nitas, exterior side panel of a
cabinet known as the Wrangel
Cabinet. 1560. Inlaid precious
woods, $27^{1}/_{2} \times 18^{1}/_{2}''$. Landesmuseum, Münster.

The earliest attempt to incorporate Renaissance elements into architecture
seems to have been this
wing of Heidelberg Castle.
Its horizontal disposition
stems from Italy, but its
somewhat excessive dec-
oration is a reinterpreta-
tion of Italian motifs done
by two Netherlanders. The
statues and reliefs make
up a typical Humanist program: Old Testament he-
roes, Roman emperors,
planetary gods, Christian
Virtues all combine to
symbolize the excellence
in war and peace of a
prince born under a lucky
star (the program is like
that of the Palazzo Schifanoia, but with Biblical
associations added). The
same taste for profuse decoration is found at Wis-
mar, an isolated outpost
of the Renaissance in the
Baltic region. Built with
record speed for a princely
marriage, there was no

time for elaborate stone carving. Except for the sandstone portal, the decoration consists mainly of polychrome terra-cotta plaques and reliefs with Renaissance motifs. The effect is not inelegant, but is neither truly Italianate, Netherlandish, nor German, and was already out of date compared with what was being done elsewhere.

Gabriel van Aken (documented 1552–61) and Valentin van Lyra (documented 1548–57). Façade, Palace of the Prince, Wismar. 1554–55. Terra-cotta decoration by Statius von Düren (documented 1550–56).

Balthasar Kircher (d. c. 1598). East side, Drapers' Hall, Brunswick. Façade completed 1591.

Antonis van Opbergen (1543–1611). The ► Great Arsenal, Danzig. 1601–5.

It was architects from the Low Countries who set the course for Germany. The Brunswick Drapers' Hall is clearly derived from the Antwerp town hall, and the whole is a happy synthesis of the notions of Vitruvius and Serlio with the Northern feeling for decoration as found in the designs of Floris, Vredeman de Vries, and Wendel Dietterlin. The richly decorated but dignified arsenal of Danzig is almost a symbol of the culture of the wealthy burghers at the century's end. The elaborate convoluted strapwork and scrollwork now seem an integral part of the building, as do the obelisks and the statues of Danzig city soldiers which here replace the Antique gods. The decorative work in stone is effectively contrasted with the brick of the walls, the two octagonal towers at the corners balance the central gables, and the building achieves an imposing air in spite of its modest dimensions. The dominating influence in all this was Vredeman de Vries whose designs for ornaments surpassed those of Floris in ingenuity. Into architectural decoration he introduced a classicizing, Humanist, moralistic note by relating the orders to the ages of man, with a complex symbolism connecting them with the type of building they were meant for.

Hans Vredeman de Vries (1527–1604). Architectural engraving from *Scenographiae, sive Perspectivae*. 1560.

Hermann Tom Ring (1521–96). Double Portrait of Ermengard and Walburg von Rietberg. 1564. Panel, 21 5/8 × 32 1/2″. Landesmuseum Münster.

In the latter half of the century, the wounds of civil and religious conflict were concealed by the luxuriousness of International Mannerism. A wealthy middle class and the aristocracy both took their standards from the Italian and French courts, and this portrait of two girls aged seven and thirteen has a disturbing resemblance to the highly sophisticated Fontainebleau portrait of the two duchesses in their bath, though this painting was done earlier. The artist belonged to a family of painters and artisans in Münster. He traveled about the Netherlands absorbing the new style, and may have got as far as England where he could have learned from Holbein's portraits. The rest of his life was spent in his modest home town doing portraits and religious pictures, city views and maps, and designs for goldsmiths, wood carvers, bookbinders, and makers of coats of arms—the uneventful career of an artist content to ply his trade within the walls of his native city. Yet even he was touched by the current which dominated all of Europe and which appealed to the taste for luxury of burghers and nobles alike.

Sigismondo, Antonio, and Bernardo Mantovano, attributed. Colonnaded court, The Residence, Landshut. c. 1536–43.

Hans Muelich (1516–73). Duke Wilhelm IV of Bavaria on His Death Bed. 1550 Panel, 13 × 9⁷/₈″. Bayerisches Nationalmuseum, Munich.

Augsburg or Munich Craftsmen. House Altar of Duke Albrecht V of Bavaria. ►
c. 1560/70. Ebony, gold, and enamel, height 24³/₄″, width shut 17⁷/₈″, width open 21¹/₈″, depth 10⁵/₈″. Schatzkammer der Residenz, Munich.

Even in Catholic Bavaria death was an obsession, and it seemed natural to have the court painter portray the moribund Duke— a startlingly realistic likeness to come from Muelich who did splendid miniatures for the manuscripts of Roland de Lassus and Cipriano de Rore, the court composers. Bavaria's was the most cosmopolitan court in Germany, and the Landshut palace is the only true Italian *palazzo* on German soil. Enamored of Giulio Romano's Palazzo del Tè, Ludwig X replaced his Augsburg architects with Mantuans. Thenceforth the Bavarian court took Italy as its ideal.

The small portable altar (p. 231) is more likely to have distracted the Duke from his private devotions than to have led him to meditate on the vanity of earthly goods. Closed, it shows the arms of Austria and Bavaria. Open, enameled-gold arabesques and jewelwork almost conceal the religious statuettes and scenes: the story of Adam and Eve in the predella; in niches Saints Anne and Albert, patrons of Duchess Anna and the Duke; directly above them other niches with allegorical figures of the Transitoriness of Life on one side, Faith on the other; and in the center the Resurrection. Jamnitzer's table ornament adapts Italian motifs to German taste. The stem consists of the Goddess of Earth on a base of plants and animals. On the basin she holds there are *putti*, plants and lizards (which, like Palissy, Jamnitzer cast directly from life), and three sirens who support a vase of flowers. All of this is done with dazzling virtuosity and imagination, and it is completely Mannerist, from the strained pose of the goddess to the lizards entwined in gold foliage. The art of engraving in rock crystal was a specialty of Milan, as we have already seen in the Albertina Casket. The Fontana workshop had a brilliant rival in that of the Saracchi brothers whose engraving has a classical perfection which, here, is beautifully contrasted by the more Mannerist gold handles and the Neptune. Ingenuity was particularly prized in the age of Mannerism. Clockwork, either in timepieces or as the motor for fantastic automata, had an irresistible fascination. The ring pictured on the following page has, in place of a jewel, a miniature watch which even—*stupore, piacere!*—strikes the hours. One can scarcely take seriously the fact that the lid of this astounding minuscule watch opens out to make an enameled-gold triptych with a Crucifixion and, on the wings, the Instruments of the Passion—even religion was part of the game of an age which indulged its every whim and could afford to, for a while at least.

◄ Augsburg Craftsman. Ring with watch (the watch by Jacob Wittmann). c. 1580. Gold and enamel, height of ring 1 1/8", diameter of watch slightly over 5/8". Schatzkammer der Residenz, Munich.

◄ Hans Raimer (d. 1604), perhaps on a design by Hans Muelich. Ornamental goblet. 1563. Enameled gold with sapphires, height 19 1/8", maximum diameter 6 3/4". Schatzkammer der Residenz, Munich.

The entire enameled-gold surface of Raimer's goblet is engraved with Moresque patterns against which stand out Italianate festoons and six cartouches, each holding a large sapphire. The Antique warrior on the lid brandishes the sapphire ring of Duchess Anna and has a sapphire buckler. But nothing surpasses the *Saint George and the Dragon.* Precious gems literally drip from it, its form dissolves in light reflected from a thousand facets or trapped in deeply glowing rubies. Even the pedestal cascades with jewels, from the arms of Bavaria at the top to the two river-goddesses below who personify—bizarrely in this context!—the virtues of Temperance and Prudence. The craftsmen of entire cities—Milan, Augsburg, Nuremberg—lived on work ordered from them by the courts of Bavaria and Prague (neither France nor the Italian principalities had wealth enough), and their bibles were the treatise on goldsmithing by Cellini and the pattern books of Du Cerceau, René Boyvin, and Étienne Delaune.

Munich Craftsmen. Saint George and the Dragon. c. 1590. Enameled gold, gilded silver, diamonds, rubies, emeralds, agate, and chalcedony, height 19 5/8", width 13 1/2", depth slightly over 7 3/4". Schatzkammer der Residenz, Munich.

Bartholomeus Spranger (1546–1611). Hercules and Omphale. Copper, $9^1/_2 \times 7^1/_2''$. Kunsthistorisches Museum, Vienna.

All this was an art infinitely remote from the "alarums and excursions" in which a world still agonized. In Prague, at the court of Rudolph II, Mannerism reached a paroxysm of sophisticated fantasy. The Emperor, intoxicated with beauty and learning, took as his ideal not Augustus but Hadrian and made of his capital not a second Rome but another Alexandria. Power politics were, for Rudolph, a game to be won by mystification and bluff, but to the end of his life he remained ignorant of the rules of the game and, so, could never

Bartholomeus Spranger. The Victory of Knowledge over Ignorance. Canvas, $64^1/_8 \times 46^1/_8''$. Kunsthistorisches Museum, Vienna.

win or even play. Like Hamlet, he walked through life willfully blind to the traps that cruder minds had set for him. It was enough for him to hide away in his *Kunst- und Wunderkammer* — his *studiolo* which far outdid that of any other prince in curiosities and works of art; or to spend his nights studying the stars in company of his court astronomers Kepler and Tycho Brahe; to lose all thought of time and place and crisis and war in the polyphony of his court composers Philippe de Monte, Jacobus de Kerle, and Jacobus Gallus; to sit for hours lost in reverie contemplating the bizarre, sensual, even lascivious canvases of his court painters Arcimboldo, Hans von Aachen, Spranger. The image of flattery which Spranger set before him was exactly what he wanted: the goddess of Wisdom, Minerva, an armored amazon whose every curve breathes impudicity, the ideal creature for the Emperor's epicene tastes, delicately tramples underfoot an ecstatic nude Ignorance, while War and Peace remain indifferent in the foreground and the Liberal Arts cluster about admiringly, brandishing the emblems of Rudolph's other two great passions, Astronomy and Geometry.

Such art was a world apart from anything preceding it in German or Netherlandish art, and nothing in Italy went quite so far in the way of superrefinement. For Cranach the theme of Hercules and Omphale was the occasion for lusty satire. For Spranger it is a study in perversity: the warrior decked in satin and jewels, the brutish crone hidden in the alcove making the sign of cuckoldry, and once again the amazon woman, a Venus in furs. Nothing in this art is virile. The figures may stand in *contrapposto*, but it is line, not weight and mass, which determines the position. The pose may seem emphatic, but as it flows along the luscious contours of the body it loses vitality and dwindles into a refined, affected gesture of the hand. Spranger's color is cool, precisely defined, bright and clear, his forms extravagant but melting in light. His first teachers in his native Antwerp implanted in him Bruegel's vein of fantasy. In a brief visit to France, he added the sensuality of Fontainebleau. Italy was decisive: in Parma he learned the luminous, otherworldly art of Correggio and Parmigianino, in Rome the tumultuous accumulation of forms of the Zuccari. From Florence he took the sinuous shapes of Giambologna and something of the madness of Rosso (the scissors-sharp profiles of the last two Arts to the right of Minerva's foot are like those in Rosso's *Daughters of Jethro*). In Cologne Hans von Aachen was trained in the Antwerp style, and in Italy underwent much the same influences as Spranger. But to these he added a Venetian feeling for tonal values and for warm, vibrant, pearly color, with forms dissolving in the shadows of a glowing sunset. Immensely versatile, he painted portraits in which the sitter stares out of the greenish shadows of a tenebrous

Hans von Aachen (1552–1615). Jupiter Embracing Antiope. Copper, 12 × 8¹/₄". Kunsthistorisches Museum, Vienna.

background, or ecstatically erotic mythological scenes, grossly laughing peasants, pious saints and naked Olympians, the sorrowing Christ and the *fêtes galantes* of the Kingdom of Venus. In Prague also was the shrewdly mad Arcimboldo who made landscapes in the form of men's heads, did surreal portraits of librarians made entirely out of books, of hunters with faces built out of game animals, of Herod with a head composed of hundreds of massacred Innocents, and even of the Emperor with a face of fruits, flowers, and vegetables, likening him to the harvest god Vertumnus who wore women's clothes to woo Pomona. Mannerism had reached its farthest limit. The artist no longer felt he had any obligation to nature. What he painted was not what

he saw but what he thought. In Prague this did not even involve painting what one felt. What counted was only the ingenuity of the "idea," the cleverness of the "conceit," the titillation of the senses in a godless delight of carnality which was never meant to be acted out in the bedchambers of reality but only dreamed about as an eternal, irresistible, unresisting temptation. The gods the Florentine Humanists had awakened from their long sleep were now no more than the bedfellows of an emperor's troubled dreams: the divinities of sunlit Olympus had returned in vain, to sleep through another age in a palace alcove. The Renaissance had ended.

Giuseppe Arcimboldo (1527–93). Fire, from a series of the Four Elements. 1566. Panel, $26^1/_8 \times 20^1/_8$". Kunsthistorisches Museum, Vienna.

All the rest is epilogue. Rudolph died, his artists drifted away, back to reality. The court sculptor Adriaen de Vries, who had studied with Giambologna and had made for Augsburg this fountain so much like the earlier Neptune fountain in Florence, went on to work at Frederiksborg and to design a mausoleum for the prince who had built the Golden Palace of Bückeburg in the late Indian summer of Mannerism. The richly carved and gilded wood decorations of that palace have a sunset glow. Fantasy takes on a new depth in the designs of Wendel Dietterlin which inspired the magnificently skillful wood carvers who worked there. This is no longer mere decoration but a kind of seething existence of the forms themselves. They become anthropomorphic: scrollwork dissolves into cartilaginous shapes, as if the human ear had been stretched, warped, uncoiled to make winding, twisting traceries which threaten to invade, of their own power, every flat surface, every bulging muscle of the gods who watch over the golden door.

Adriaen de Vries (c. 1560–1627). The Hercules Fountain (detail). 1596–1602. Bronze. Augsburg.

Eckbert Wolff the Younger (documented 1591–1608/9). Altar Table. 1601–4. Gilded wood. Palace Chapel, Bückeburg.

Eckbert Wolff the Younger, ▶ attributed. Door of the Gods in the Golden Hall of the Palace, Bückeburg. c. 1605–8. Polychromed and gilded wood.

Hubert Gerhard (c. 1550–1620).
Angel with Baptismal Font. 1596.
Bronze, height 70⅞″. Sankt Michael, Munich.

Friedrich Sustris (1524–99) with ►
Wolfgang Miller and Wendel Dietrich. Interior, Sankt Michael,
Munich. 1583–97.

In religious art it was as if all the excesses that partisanship had led to were now brought under control. Art in Bavaria took on a Roman gravity in which neither fantasy nor ecstasy had a place. Gerhard had left the Netherlands to study with Giambologna in Florence, then settled in southern Germany. The lessons of his master remained with him, but in the last years of the century there came into his style a massiveness and solemnity which are more Baroque than Mannerist, and which reflect the sober dignity of the Jesuit church of Sankt Michael where he worked in Munich. That church was built for the Jesuits by Duke Wilhelm V to commemorate the victory of the Counter Reformation in Bavaria. Its model was the recently erected Gesù

in Rome, the chief seat of the Jesuits. The keynote of Sankt Michael, as of the Gesù, is the power of a Church which had been challenged, had done battle, and emerged reduced but still mighty. What was needed now was a church to which the faithful could turn for guidance, a church designed for preaching. So, like the Gesù, Sankt Michael has a single vast barrel-vaulted nave with the pulpit close to the congregation. Its proportions are noble, its decoration rich but austere, its character grandiose. There is nothing here of the mystical gloom of Gothic cathedrals, nor is there the sunlit serenity and human measure of the Early Renaissance churches of Brunelleschi. Those eras were ended. No longer was either God or man the measure, but the unshakable authority of the Church itself. Man had embarked upon the Renaissance confident of his own powers to think and to create. He had survived the age of Mannerism when doubts had assailed him, when he had fled from uncertainty into a world of fantasy or else joined battle against the powers of earth and Heaven, and he had made of that age as audacious an exploration of the labyrinth of the soul as the Renaissance's exploration of the worlds of the past and the present. Now, in a new age, known in art as the Baroque, he was to go on to consolidate his conquests, to achieve a new and more masterful relationship with the world about him, and to prepare the way to a future even more beset with problems than had been the past.

Elias Holl (1573–1646). The Arsenal, Augsburg. 1602–7. On the façade, Hans Reichle (c. 1570–1642), The Archangel Michael, 1603–6, bronze statue group.

Peter de Witte, known as ▶ Pietro Candido (c. 1548–1628), attributed. Portrait of Duchess Magdalena of Bavaria. 1613? Panel, $38^3/_8 \times 28^1/_8$". Alte Pinakothek, Munich.

Mannerism refused the natural laws of gravity, of structure, of human character and appearance. No form rests where it should in this façade, nothing begun is completed. The surface is broken nervously by projections and recesses which aim at coloristic effects, pediments are interrupted to frame but not form oval windows which are held up by no more than an ineffectual triglyph. Reichle's Saint Michael is poised in space, the prostrate Satan would pitch downward if he were not held fast by the archangel who himself seems to have no weight. The statue gyrates in violence, a bronze flame poised dangerously on a façade whose forms are unstable. It is as if the idea of both the statue and the building were a moment's fancy, the instant frozen forever in bronze and stone, impermanence constrained into permanence. And so it is with the portrait too. Nervous, apprehensive, the Duchess will be prisoner forever in her pyramid of jewels. The trappings of power will weigh unbearably, the hand tire but never move, the heavy lids never sleep. The creatures of the Renaissance, too, were suspended in time. But their time was an infinity of repose in which man was the balanced center of a balanced world. In a world which cracked and crumbled beneath men's feet, Mannerist time was an uncertain instant intolerably prolonged.

ANNO · ETATIS ·   · SVÆ · XLIX ·

ENGLAND

In England the break with Rome crippled art for a century, though the ambition of Henry VIII was to be a Renaissance prince, a Maecenas of the arts as well as a warrior. The workshops of Nottingham ceased to produce the exquisite alabaster religious images which for centuries had been coveted by churches from Spain to Scandinavia. The superbly imaginative Perpendicular Gothic style in architecture was meant for churches, but no new churches were built. The link with the past was broken, and in the visual arts there was no one to forge a new one, not even the Italians, Netherlanders, and Germans Henry summoned to his service. There was an extraordinary release in music, poetry, and the theater. Not so in the visual arts. Even Holbein had little immediate influence, though it was in England that he became one of the greatest of all portraitists. He was simply not strong enough to bring about, singlehanded, a Renaissance in a spiritually divided country.

◄ Hans Holbein the Younger. Portrait of Henry VIII. 1540? Panel, 32½ × 29″ (replica). Galleria Nazionale, Rome.

Hans Holbein the Younger (designed by). Casing for a late-medieval rock-crystal bowl. c. 1540. Rock crystal, gold, enameled gold, pearls, and semiprecious stones, height 6¼″, diameter 7½″. Schatzkammer der Residenz, Munich.

247

◀ Anonymous. Portrait of Queen Elizabeth I (the so-called Cobham Portrait). c. 1591. Canvas, 43³/₄ × 30¹/₂″. National Portrait Gallery, London.

Hans Eworth (1520–73). Portrait of Henry Stuart, Lord Darnley, and His Brother Charles Stuart, Earl of Lennox. 1563. Panel, 25 × 15″. Windsor Castle.

When the young Elizabeth came to the throne in 1558, it was more than conventional court flattery to acclaim her as Astraea, the goddess heralding a new Golden Age. Divinely unpredictable, as much victim as mistress of her whims, she gave new impetus to the arts through her own passionate enthusiasms. Her early portraits still show her in human guise. Later, after the victory over the Spanish Armada, she became a cult image, an icon of royal authority in which the pinched features and thin body almost disappear behind the show of majesty, and it was those portraits that she distributed as pledges of loyalty and tokens of favor. England opened itself to foreign influences. Italian litterateurs flocked to London, bringing with them a Renaissance culture which was outdated but so much the more exciting for its tang of Mannerist passion and mystery which struck fire in a Marlowe or a Shakespeare. Italian painters came and also Netherlanders. The stereotyped court portrait took on new character, as in this likeness of the two young brothers. Eworth had begun his English career around 1545 with portraits as sober as those of Mor and Holbein. But then, in Elizabeth's reign, a new vein of Mannerist fantasy was fostered by the alembicated allegories of the poets who clustered about her. Here, though the hall that serves as a background is probably a realistic representation of a palace interior of the time, it has been placed off-angle to create a feeling of the mystery of vast space behind the sharp silhouettes of the two youngsters. One uniquely English, almost Shakespearian art form was developed at that time, chiefly by Nicholas Hilliard and Isaac Oliver: the portrait miniature. In it the likeness of a passion-torn nobleman might be set before a background of flames, or posed behind a screen of white roses, languidly leaning on a tree, hand on heart, for all the world like the lovesick swain in *As You Like It*.

Sir John Thynne (d. 1580) and Robert Smythson (1536?–1614). Longleat House, Warminster, Wiltshire. 1567–80.

Robert Lyming. Garden façade, Hatfield House, ▶ Hertfordshire. 1611.

Restless with unsatisfied human desires, the spinster Queen traveled about the country to visit her nobles, always with a large retinue which had to be housed, fed, and entertained with masques and revels and hunts, all at the expense of the unfortunate, though flattered, nobleman. But from this grew a new feeling for commodious living, and the old castles were replaced by comfortable manor houses. At Longleat the basic notions of Italy were adopted, though it still lacks the juxtaposition of bold masses and the emphasis on the portal. Its style is eclectic, with features borrowed from Serlio, Palladio, De Vries, and Du Cerceau, and Sir John's conservative neighbors mocked at him for his preoccupation with decorative details. Hatfield House has the same eclecticism, but a U-plan replaces the traditional English H-plan, and this makes of it a more comfortable dwelling without the wasted space and expense of extended wings. Its arcaded stone façade, with openwork balustrades like those of Philibert Delorme, strikes an Italian note in contrast with the Netherlandish brickwork of the wings.

Anonymous. Tomb of Princess Mary (detail). c. 1607. Polychromed alabaster. Chapel of Henry VII, Westminster Abbey, London.

So strong was the English tradition of funeral monuments that even Pietro Torrigiani, summoned from Florence by Henry VIII to build a tomb for his father in the new style, gave a Gothic cast to his figures, though he surrounded them with the ubiquitous *putti* of Italy. Well on into the century, tombs continued to be set into wall niches or were simple slabs with the effigy stretched out stiffly in the medieval manner. Later there was a peculiarly English innovation. Semirealistic figures in alabaster or freestone were painted in oils with waxy, warmly tinted flesh and bright and even garish colors for the garments. A show of life was given to these effigies by having them either kneel or else recline, propped up on one elbow, as here where the child princess seems to look on with envy at the world of the living. For the pedestals and settings of the tombs, varicolored marbles and painted alabaster were used, and the ornamental designs were often borrowed from Vredefman de Vries, Du Cerceau, or the Italians. As elsewhere, then, foreign influences were at last incorporated in a happy union with a native expression to create an art at one and the same time national and international.

Whatever criteria may be adopted, and there are others than those set out in these pages, it is evident that there came about, at the start of the fifteenth century, two Renaissances of comparable importance, one in Italy, the other in the Low Countries. The worlds they represented could not be more unlike. Italian art was first an expression of a patrician republican city and of small principalities, each of which had its own character, its own intellectual leaders, its own artists. It was also the expression of the populace, on the one hand through artisans ever alert to innovations, on the other hand through a church in which nobles and plebeians were nnited in a single, unquestioned creed. When, later, the one universal power in Italy, Papal Rome, joined in the new movement, there were new ambitions and a grandiosity in contrast with the most elementary original principle of the Renaissance, that man is the measure of all things. But by that time the world itself was changing in an unpredictable direction which would give rise to a quite different art. As for the Low Countries, there a middle class, wealthy or modest, set the course for a less intellectual, more down-to-earth art than Italy's. And there too, when the accidents of history brought an ambitious emperor to the throne, new ambitions set off new trends. But the flames that had been lighted in Germany quickly set all in question. The art which arose then was the most contradictory phenomenon in history. The high achievements of the great centers and the tentative gropings of the tributary centers were all forced into the single mainstream of International Mannerism—a universal style whose one consistent characteristic was an incredible diversity of highly personal, individualistic expressions. Renaissance art had aimed at unity, congruity, rationalism, clarity, proportion, harmony. Mannerist art exploited diversity, contrast, illogicality, obscurantism, eroticism, disproportion, dissonance. It had a single goal: to be expressive. Expressiveness might take the form of fantastic ornamentation in a free play of surface appearances. It could also be the product of individual vision and sensibility, of one man's doubt and emotional confusion. What unified all was the effect on the spectator—*fare piacere, fare stupore*, to give pleasure, to astound.

Pietro Torrigiani (1472–1528). Tomb of Henry VII and Elizabeth of York (detail). 1512–18. Bronze. Chapel of Henry VII, Westminster Abbey, London.

From Renaissance to Mannerism 1400-1600: Centers and Schools

Between Gothic and Renaissance

Early Renaissance

1400	10	20	30	40

FLORENCE   Republic   The Medici: Cosimo the Elder

Ghiberti, Nanni di Banco, Donatello, Brunelleschi, Masolino, Masaccio   Uccello, Filippo Lippi, Alberti, *Domenico Venezia*

Gentile da Fabriano, Angelico, Luca della Robbia, Castagno, Desider

---

SIENA   Jacopo della Quercia   *Ghiberti, Donatello*   Sassetta, Giovanni di Paolo,

FERRARA   The Este: Lionello

Pisanello, J. Bellini, *Rogier van d*

UMBRIA and SOUTHERN TUSCANY   Piero della Francesca

RIMINI

URBINO

MILAN   The Sforza

ROME   Pope Martin V   Eugenius IV   Nicholas

Masolino   Filarete

Masaccio   Fra Angel.

Gentile da Fabriano, Pisanello

VENICE and its MAINLAND   Pisanello, Jacopo Bellini, *Uccello, Filippo Lippi*   *Castagno, Donate*

FLANDERS   John the Fearless   Philip the Good

and BRABANT   Robert Campin ("Master of Flémalle"), Jan van Eyck, Rogier van der Weyden

---

ARAGON and CASTILLE

FRANCE

Renaissance   Mannerism   Between Mannerism
                                        and Baroque

| 60 | 70 | 80 | 90 | 1500 |

Lorenzo the Magnificent

ino da Fiesole, Antonio and Bernardo Rossellini, Agostino di Duccio, Pollaiuolo, Ghirlandaio, Filippino Lippi, Torrigiani
ichelozzo, Gozzoli, Verrocchio, Benedetto and Guiliano da Maiano, Giuliano da Sangallo, Botticelli, Piero di Cosimo, Cronaca

Leonardo da Vinci   Michelangelo

atteo di Giovanni, Vecchietta, Neroccio de' Landi, Francesco di Giorgio Martini, Benvenuto di Giovanni

rso   Ercole I

eyden, Pannonio, Piero della Francesca, Cossa, Tura, De' Roberti, Rossetti

Pinturicchio, Perugino, Signorelli, Raphael

gismondo Malatesta
ederigo da Montefeltro
berti, Agostino di Duccio   Laurana, Bramante
ero della Francesca   Melozzo da Forlì, *Justus of Ghent, P. Berruguete*

ancesco   Galeazzo   Lodovico il Moro and Beatrice d'Este
arete   Mantegazza, Foppa   Amadeo, Briosco, *Bramante, Leonardo,* De Predis

MANTUA   The Gonzaga: Lodovico   Francesco II and Isabella d'Este
               Alberti   *Mantegna*

Pius II   Paul II   Sixtus IV   Innocent VIII   Alexander VI
                        Bregno, Mino da Fiesole   *Botticelli, Signorelli, Perugino, Pinturicchio*
                        Dalmata, Melozzo da Forlì   *Pollaiuolo*
                                                           Giuliano da Sangallo

e Vivarini, Crivelli, Mantegna, Gentile and Giovanni Bellini, Pietro Lombardo, Codussi, Carpaccio, Cima, Montagna
               Antonello da Messina, Verrocchio, Jacopo de' Barbari, *Dürer*

Charles the Bold
D. Bouts   Hugo van der Goes, Memling   Gerard David

NORTH NETHERLANDS   Hieronymus Bosch

Ferdinand and Isabella
Dalmau   Bermejo   P. Berruguete   *A. Sansovino*

Charles VII   Louis XI   Charles VIII
LOIRE VALLEY: Fouquet   *Master of Moulins,* Bourdichon, Colombe

NUREMBERG and INNSBRUCK   Maximilian I
               Muscat, Veit Stoss, Vischer the Elder

WÜRZBURG   Riemenschneider

255

	1500	10	20	30	40

FLORENCE — Duke Alessandro — Cosimo I, Grand Duke of Tusca[ny]
Fra Bartolomeo, Sarto, *Alonso Berruguete*, Rosso — Michelangelo, Pontormo — Bandinelli, Bronzino, Vasa[ri]
Leonardo, Raphael

SIENA
Sodoma — Beccafumi, Marco Pino

FERRARA (Alfonso I d'Este) — **PARMA** (the Farnese) and **MODENA** (the Este)
Dosso and Battista Dossi, Garofalo — Correggio, Parmigianino, Mazzola Bedoli, Dell'Abbate

MANTUA (Federico II Gonzaga) *Giulio Romano, Primaticcio*

MILAN, LOMBARDY, GENOA
Bramantino, *Leonardo*, Gaudenzio Ferrari, Luini, Cristoforo Lombardo, Pordenone

VENICE
Giorgione, *Dürer*, Tullio Lombardo, Lorenzo Lotto, Moretto, Titian, Serlio, Sanmicheli, J. Sansovino — Schiavone, Titian

ROME — Julius II — Leo X — Clement VII — Paul III
Bramante, A. Sansovino, *Raphael*, Giulio Romano — *Cellini, Giovanni da Udine* — Heemskerck, *F. Floris, Daniele da Volter*[ra]
Peruzzi, Michelangelo, Sebastiano del Piombo, Raimondi, *Scorel* — Michelangelo, Perin del Vaga, Salviati, P[...]

SPAIN — Charles V
Plateresque Style — SEVILLE: *Torrigiani* — GRANADA: Siloe, Machuca — SEVILLE: *Pedro*
Juan de Flandes — VALENCIA: Macip, Yáñez, Juanes — Mora
CASTILLE: A. Berruguete, *Juan de Juni*

FRANCE — Louis XII — François I — Henri
— Cather[ine]
The Giusti, Mazzoni — *Leonardo* FONTAINEBLEAU: *Penni, Rosso, Primaticcio, Cellini, Serlio*
Domenico da Cortona, G. della Robbia, Sarto — Le Breton, Jean Clouet, Pierre Bontemps
PARIS: Léonard Limousin, Lescot, Delor[me]

NORTH NETHERLANDS
Gossaert, Lucas van Leyden — *Vincidor* — UTRECHT: Jan van Scorel
HAARLEM: Maerten van Heemsker[ck]

MALINES and IMPERIAL TERRITORY — Margaret of Austria, Regent
J. de' Barbari, Meit, Mone, *Vincidor*, Orley

ANTWERP
Metsijs — Antwerp "Mannerists," Patinir, Swart van Groeningen, Hemessen, P. Bruegel, Aertsen

NUREMBERG
Dürer, *J. de' Barbari*, Veit Stoss, Vischer the Younger, Peter Flötner, Barthel and Sebald Beham, Pencz

WÜRZBURG — MUNICH — Ludwig X — Wilhelm IV
Riemenschneider — Dell — *The Mantovani*, Refinger

AUGSBURG — The Fuggers and the Imperial Court
Holbein the Elder, Burgkmair, Daucher, Hering — Amberger, *Tit*[...]

RHINELAND — Wydyz, Matthias Grünewald, Holbein the Younger, Baldung Grien

DANUBE SCHOOL
Cranach the Elder, Preu, Altdorfer, Huber

WITTENBERG — The Electors of Saxony
Cranach the Elder, *Meit, Dürer, J. de' Barbari* — Crana[ch]

ENGLAND — Henry VIII — M[...]
Torrigiani — *Holbein the Younger*

Francesco I   Ferdinando I

lviati, Cellini, Ammannati, Giambologna, Cavalori, Maso, Giovanni dell'Opera, Santi di Tito, Butteri, Poppi, Buontalenti
Stradano, F. Sustris, E. de Witte, A. de Vries, P. de Witte, J. Bilivert, Alessandro Allori

BOLOGNA   *Calvaert,* the Carracci, Guido Reni

Lelio Orsi, Bertoia, *Spranger*

Leoni, Alessi, Tibaldi, Arcimboldo, Cambiaso, A. Fontana, the Saracchi, Lomazzo

copo Bassano, Jacopo Tintoretto, Veronese, Vittoria, Palladio, Scamozzi   *Hans von Aachen,* Palma the Younger

lius III   Paul IV   Pius IV   Pius V   Gregory XIII   Sixtus V
Ammannati, T. Zuccari   A. Lippi, *Spranger, F. Zuccari, Barocci, A. de Vries*   Caravaggio
Vasari, Vignola   *P. Bril, Elsheimer*

Philip II

ampaña   ESCORIAL: J. B. de Toledo, Herrera   *Cambiaso, Tibaldi*
             P. Leoni, *Mor,* Coello, Navarrete   *F. Zuccari*
                    CASTILLE: Beltrán   TOLEDO: *El Greco*

d   Charles IX   Henri III   Henri IV and
Medici   Marie de Medici
lviati, Dell'Abbate, *Spranger*   *Dubois,* Dubreuil, Fréminet
an Cousin, François Clouet, Antoine Caron
an Goujon, Germain Pilon, Du Cerceau, Bernard Palissy   LORRAINE: Bellange

Bosschaert, Bloemaert, Wttewael
Mander, Ketel, Goltzius, Cornelisz van Haarlem

Anthonis Mor, Cornelis Floris, Maerten de Vos, Vredeman de Vries   Coninxloo, J. Bruegel

                            NORTH GERMANY   *Vredeman de Vries,* Ring, *Floris, A. de Vries*
    Jamnitzer   and SCANDINAVIA   Wolff, *Opbergen,* Steenwinkel

brecht V   Wilhelm V
         Raimer, Muelich   *F. Sustris, Gerhard, P. de Witte, Dietterlin*

                                             A. de Vries, Gerhard, Reichle, Holl

PRAGUE   Rudolph II
                 Spranger, Arcimboldo, Heintz, A. de Vries, Hans von Aachen

e Younger

udor   Elizabeth I
    Mor   Eworth   Hilliard   *F. Zuccari*   Oliver

Bibliography

In a field so vast, one can give no more than a few hints for further reading. Studies on individual artists have been included only if they treat of the period in general or concern artists not adequately discussed elsewhere. Much information can be gained from exhibition catalogues, always a fruitful, objective source.

AESTHETICS AND CULTURAL HISTORY

BAROCCHI, P., *Trattati d'arte del Cinquecento*, Bari, 1960-62, 3 vols.

BATTISTI, E., *L'Antirinascimento*, Milan, 1962

BATTISTI, E., *Rinascimento e Barocco*, Milan, 1960

BAUMGART, F., *Renaissance und Kunst des Manierismus*, Cologne, 1963

BENESCH, O., *The Art of the Renaissance in Northern Europe*, Cambridge, Mass., 1947

Between Renaissance and Mannerism, exhibition catalogue, Manchester, 1965

BLUNT, A., *Artistic Theory in Italy 1450-1600*, Oxford, 1962

BURCKHARDT, J., *The Civilization of the Renaissance in Italy* [1860], New York, 1929

CASSIRER, E., *The Individual and the Cosmos in Renaissance Philosophy,* New York, 1964

CHASTEL, A., and KLEIN, R., *The Age of Humanism*, New York, 1964

DVŎRÁK, M., *Kunstgeschichte als Geistesgeschichte*, Munich, 1924

GILMORE, M., *The World of Humanism 1453-1517*, New York, 1952

GOMBRICH, E. H., *Norm and Form, Studies in the Art of the Renaissance*, London, 1966

HAY, D., ed., *The Age of the Renaissance*, New York, 1967

HOLT, E. G., *A Documentary History of Art*, New York, 1957, 2 vols.

HUIZINGA, J., *The Waning of the Middle Ages*, New York, 1954

KLEIN, R., and ZERNER, H., *Italian Art 1500-1600, Sources and Documents*, New Jersey, 1966

Le seizième siècle européen, exhibition catalogue, Paris, 1965, 4 vols.

L'Europe humaniste, exhibition catalogue, Brussels, 1954

KRISTELLER, P. O., *Renaissance Thought*, New York, 1961, 2 vols.

MANDER, K. VAN, *Dutch and Flemish Painters* [1604], tr. C. van de Wall, New York, 1936

MESNIL, J., *L'Art au nord et au sud des Alpes à l'époque de la Renaissance*, Paris, 1911

MONTANO, R., *L'Estetica del Rinascimento e del Barocco*, Naples, 1962

PANOFSKY, E., *Idea, ein Beitrag zur Begriffsgeschichte der älteren Kunsttheorie*, Leipzig-Berlin, 1924

PANOFSKY, E., *Meaning in the Visual Arts*, New York, 1957

PANOFSKY, E., *Renaissance and Renascences*, Stockholm, 1966

PANOFSKY, E., *Studies in Iconology*, New York, 1962

SÁNCHEZ-CANTÓN, F. J., *Fuentes literarias para la historia del arte español*, Madrid, 1923, 1933, 2 vols.

SCHLOSSER-MAGNINO, J., *La Letteratura artistica*, rev. ed., Florence, 1964

SEZNEC, J., *The Survival of the Pagan Gods*, New York, 1953

SHEARMAN, J., *Mannerism*, Baltimore, 1967

SYMONDS, J. A., *Renaissance in Italy* [1900], New York, 1960, 2 vols.

SYPHER, W., *Four Stages in Renaissance Style*, New York, 1955

Triomphe du Maniérisme, exhibition catalogue, Amsterdam, 1955

VASARI, G., *The Lives of the Painters, Sculptors and Architects* [1568], tr. by A. B. Hinds, New York, 1927, 4 vols.

WIND, E., *Pagan Mysteries in the Renaissance*, rev. ed., Baltimore, 1967

WÖLFFLIN, H., *Renaissance and Baroque* [1888], London, 1964

WÜRTENBERGER, F., *Mannerism*, New York, 1963

SPECIAL STUDIES

CLARK, K., *Landscape into Art*, Boston, Mass., 1961

CLARK, K., *The Nude*, New York, 1961

FORSSMAN, E., *Säule und Ornament*, Stockholm, 1956

JACQUOT, J., ed., *Fêtes et cérémonies au temps de Charles-Quint*, Paris, 1960

JACQUOT, J., ed., *Les Fêtes de la Renaissance*, Paris, 1956

JOBÉ, J., ed., *Great Tapestries*, Lausanne, 1965

KRIS, E., *Steinschneidekunst*, Vienna, 1929, 2 vols.

MÜLLER, T., *Sculpture in the Netherlands, Germany, France, and Spain 1400-1500*, Baltimore, 1966

PANOFSKY, E., *Tomb Sculpture*, New York, 1964

PEVSNER, N., *An Outline of European Architecture*, rev. ed., Baltimore, 1963

POPE-HENNESSY, J., *The Portrait in the Renaissance*, Princeton, 1967

Schatzkammer der Residenz, museum catalogue, Munich, 1963

SINGER, C., *A Short History of Anatomy*, New York, 1957

WHITE, J., *The Birth and Rebirth of Pictorial Space*, London, 1957

WITTKOWER, R., *Architectural Principles in the Age of Humanism*, rev. ed., London, 1962

ITALY

Arte Lombarda dai Visconti agli Sforza, exhibition catalogue, Milan, 1958

BECHERUCCI, L., *Manieristi toscani*, Bergamo, 1944

BERENSON, B., *Italian Pictures of the Renaissance, Florentine School*, London, 1963, 2 vols.

BERENSON, B., *Italian Pictures of the Renaissance, Venetian School*, London, 1957, 2 vols.

BERENSON, B., *The Drawings of the Florentine Painters*, Chicago, 1938, 3 vols.

BODMER, H., *Correggio und die Maler der Emilia*, Vienna, 1942; Italian ed., Novara, 1943

BORSOOK, E., *Mural Painters of Tuscany*, London, 1960

BRIGANTI, G., *Il Manierismo e Pellegrino Tibaldi*, Rome, 1945

BRIGANTI, G., *Italian Mannerism*, Dresden, 1962

Carlo Crivelli e i Crivelleschi, exhibition catalogue, Venice, 1961

CHASTEL, A., *Art et humanisme à Florence au temps de Laurent le Magnifique*, Paris, 1959

CHASTEL, A., *Italian Art*, New York, 1963

CHASTEL. A., *The Flowering of the Italian Renaissance*, New York, 1965

CHASTEL, A., *The Studios and Styles of the Italian Renaissance*, New York, 1966

CROWE, J. A., and CAVALCASELLE, G. B., *A History of Painting in Italy*, London, 1903–14, 6 vols.

CROWE, J. A., and CAVALCASELLE, G. B., *A History of Painting in North Italy*, New York, 1912, 3 vols.

DAVIES, M., *London National Gallery: Earlier Italian Schools*, New York, 1951, 2 vols.

Decorative Arts of the Italian Renaissance 1400–1600, exhibition catalogue, Detroit, 1958–59

FREEDBERG, S. J., *Painting of the High Renaissance in Rome and Florence*, Cambridge, Mass., 1961, 2 vols.

FRIEDLAENDER, W., *Mannerism and Anti-Mannerism in Italian Painting*, New York, 1957

Giorgione e i Giorgioneschi, exhibition catalogue, Venice, 1955

GOULD, C., *An Introduction to Italian Renaissance Painting*, London, 1957

GOULD, C., *National Gallery Catalogues: Sixteenth Century Venetian School*, London, 1959

GOULD, C., *National Gallery Catalogues: The Sixteenth Century Italian Schools (excluding the Venetian)*, London, 1962

Italian Bronze Statuettes, exhibition catalogue, London, 1961

Jacopo Bassano, exhibition catalogue, Venice, 1957

Juste de Gand, Berruguete et la cour d'Urbino, exhibition catalogue, Ghent, 1957

LONGHI, R., *Officina Ferrarese*, Florence, 1956

Lorenzo Lotto, exhibition catalogue, Venice, 1952

MASSON, G., *Italian Gardens*, New York, 1961

MASSON, G., *Italian Villas and Palaces*, New York, 1959

MAZZOTTI, G., *Ville Venete*, Rome, 1966

MURRAY, P., *The Architecture of the Italian Renaissance*, London, 1963

Pontormo e il primo manierismo fiorentino, exhibition catalogue, Florence, 1956

POPE-HENNESSY, J., *Italian High Renaissance and Baroque Sculpture*, London, 1963, 3 vols.

POPE-HENNESSY, J., *Italian Renaissance Sculpture*, London, 1958

POPE-HENNESSY, J., *Sienese Quattrocento Painting*, New York, 1957

RACKHAM, B., *Italian Maiolica*, London, 1952

ROSSI, F., *Italian Jeweled Arts*, New York, 1957

SCHUBRING, P., *Cassoni, Truhen und Truhenbilder*, Leipzig, 1923, 2 vols.

SEYMOUR, C., *Sculpture in Italy 1400–1500*, Baltimore, 1966

TIETZE, H., and TIETZE-CONRAT, E., *The Drawings of the Venetian Painters in the 15th and 16th Centuries*, New York, 1944

TOLNAY, C. DE, *Michelangelo*, Princeton, 1947–60, 5 vols. to date

Vasari e la sua cerchia, exhibition catalogue, Florence, 1964

WÖLFFLIN, H., *Classic Art* [1899], Greenwich, Conn., 1953

ZERI, F., *Pittura e Controriforma*, Turin, 1957

SPAIN

AZCÁRATE, J. M., *Escultura del siglo XVI*, Madrid, 1958

BOSQUE, A. DE, *Artistes italiens en Espagne du XIVe siècle aux Rois Catholiques*, Paris, 1965

Carlos V y su ambiente, exhibition catalogue, Toledo, 1958

El Escorial, Madrid, 1963, 2 vols.

GOITIA-MORENO, M. F., *Las Águilas del Renacimiento español*, Madrid, 1941

IÑÍGUEZ, D. A., *Pintura del Renacimiento*, Madrid, 1954

KUBLER, G., and SORIA, M., *Art and Architecture in Spain and Portugal and their American Dominions 1500–1800*, Baltimore, 1966

PERERA, J. H., *Escultores florentinos en España*, Madrid, 1957

POST, C. R., *A History of Spanish Painting*, Cambridge, Mass., 1947–66, vols. 9–14

FRANCE

BÉGUIN, S., *L'École de Fontainebleau*, Paris, 1960

BLUNT, A., *Art and Architecture in France 1500–1700*, rev. ed., Baltimore, 1957

DIMIER, L., *French Painting in the 16th Century*, New York, 1911

DIMIER, L., *Histoire de la peinture de portrait en France au 16e siècle*, Paris, 1924–26, 2 vols.

FÉLICE, R. DE, *Le Meuble français du moyen âge à Louis XIII*, Paris, 1922

FONTAINE, G., *La Céramique française*, Paris, 1946

Fontainebleau e la maniera italiana, exhibition catalogue, Naples, 1952

GÉBELIN, F., *Les Châteaux de la Renaissance*, Paris, 1927

NOEL, J.-F., and JAHAN, P., *Les Gisants*, Paris, 1948

PANOFSKY, E., and PANOFSKY, D., "The Iconography of the Galerie François Ier at Fontainebleau," in *Gazette des Beaux-Arts*, 52, Paris, 1958

RING, G., *A Century of French Painting 1400–1500*, Greenwich, Conn., 1949

STERLING, C., and ADHÉMAR, H., *Musée du Louvre: La Peinture de l'école française, 14e–16e siècles*, catalogue, Paris, 1965

YATES, F., *The French Academies of the 16th Century*, London, 1949

THE LOW COUNTRIES

BERGSTRÖM, I., *Dutch Still-Life Painting in the 17th Century*, New York, 1956

Charles V et son temps, exhibition catalogue, Ghent, 1955

DAVIES, M., *London National Gallery: Early Netherlandish School*, New York, 1955

DELBANCO, G., *Der Maler Abraham Bloemart,* Strasbourg, 1928

Die Frankenthaler Maler, exhibition catalogue, Mannheim, 1962

Fiamminghi e Italia, exhibition catalogue, Bruges-Venice-Rome, 1951

Flanders in the 15th Century, exhibition catalogue, Detroit, 1960

Flemish Art 1300–1700, exhibition catalogue, London, 1953

Fleurs et jardins dans l'art flamand, exhibition catalogue, Ghent, 1960

FRIEDLÄNDER, M. J., *Altniederländische Malerei,* Berlin-Leiden, 1924–37, 14 vols.

GERSON, H., and KUILE, E. H. TER, *Art and Architecture in Belgium 1600–1800,* Baltimore, 1960

HEDICKE, R., *Cornelis Floris und die Florisdecoration.* Berlin, 1911, 2 vols.

Jan Gossaert genaamd Mabuse, exhibition catalogue, Rotterdam-Bruges, 1965

Jan van Scorel, exhibition catalogue, Utrecht, 1955

KAUFFMANN, H., "Der Manierismus in Holland und die Schule von Fontainebleau," in *Jahrbuch der preussischen Kunstsammlungen,* 44, 1923

L'Art flamand dans les collections espagnoles, exhibition catalogue, Bruges, 1958

LAVALLEYE, J., *Bruegel and Lucas van Leyden: Complete Engravings, Etchings, and Woodcuts,* New York, 1967

Le Paysage aux Pays-Bas de Bruegel à Rubens, 1550–1630, exhibition catalogue, Ghent, 1961

Le Siècle de Bruegel, exhibition catalogue, Brussels, 1963

LINDEMAN, C. M. A. A., *Joachim Anthonisz Wttewael,* Utrecht, 1929

Marguerite d'Autriche, exhibition catalogue, Malines, 1958

MICHEL, E., *Musée du Louvre: Peintures flamandes du XVe et du XVIe siècle,* Paris, 1953

PANOFSKY, E., *Early Netherlandish Painting,* Cambridge, Mass., 1953, 2 vols.

PUYVELDE, L. VAN, *La Peinture flamande au siècle de Bosch et Bruegel,* Paris, 1962

PUYVELDE, L. VAN, *Les Primitifs flamands,* Brussels, 1954

ROSENBERG, J., SLIVE, S., and KUILE, E. H. TER, *Dutch Art and Architecture 1600–1800,* Baltimore, 1966

VERMEULEN, F. A. J., *Handboek tot de Geschiedenis der Nederlandsche Bouwkunst,* The Hague, 1931, vol. 3

WILENSKI, R. H., *Flemish Painters 1430–1830,* London, 1960, 2 vols.

GERMANY

Aufgang der Neuzeit 1500–1650, exhibition catalogue, Nuremberg, 1952

BURGER, F., SCHMITZ, H., and BETH, I., *Die deutsche Malerei vom ausgehenden Mittelalter bis zum Ende der Renaissance,* Potsdam, 1918–19, 3 vols.

Die Kunst der Donauschule 1490–1540, exhibition catalogue, Sankt Florian and Linz, 1965

Die Malerfamilie Holbein in Basel, exhibition catalogue, Basel, 1960

DIEZ, E., "Der Hofmaler Bartholomeus Spranger," in *Jahrb. d. Kunst. d. Allerhöchsten Kaiserhauses,* XXVIII, 1909

FEULNER, A., and MÜLLER, T., *Geschichte der deutschen Plastik,* Munich, 1953

FISCHER, O., *Deutsche Zeichnung und Graphik,* Munich, 1951

German Art 1400–1800, exhibition catalogue, Manchester, 1961

Hans Baldung Grien, exhibition catalogue, Karlsruhe, 1959

Hans Holbein der Ältere und die Kunst der Spätgotik, exhibition catalogue, Augsburg, 1965

HERAMIN, F., *Gli artisti italiani in Germania,* Rome, 1935, 3 vols.

KNAPPE, K. A., *Dürer: Complete Engravings, Etchings, and Woodcuts,* New York, 1965

Meister um Dürer, exhibition catalogue, Nuremberg, 1961

MÖLLER, L., *Der Wrangelschrank und die verwandten süddeutschen Intarsienmöbel des 16. Jahrhunderts,* Berlin, 1956

PANOFSKY, E., *Albrecht Dürer,* Princeton, 1955, 2 vols.

PELTZER, R. A., "Der Hofmaler Hans von Aachen," in *Jahrb. d. Kunst. Samml. d. Allerhöchsten Kaiserhauses,* XXX, 1912

STEINBART, K., "Niederländische Hofmaler der Bairischen Herzöge," in *Marburger Jahrbuch für Kunstwissenschaft,* 4, 1928

ENGLAND

GANZ, P., *The Paintings of Hans Holbein,* Greenwich, Conn., 1956

MERCER, E., *English Art 1553–1625,* New York, 1962

POPE-HENNESSY, J., "Nicholas Hilliard and Mannerist Art Theory," in *Journal of the Warburg and Courtauld Institutes,* 6, 1943

SUMMERSON, J., *Architecture in Britain 1530–1830,* Baltimore, 1953

WATERHOUSE, E., K. *Painting in Britain 1530–1790,* Baltimore, 1953

WHINNEY, M., *Sculpture in Britain 1530–1830,* Baltimore, 1964

WINTER, C., *Elizabethan Miniatures,* Baltimore, 1956

Index

Photo credits: Alinari, Florence, front and back end papers, p. 13, 14, 29 lower, 30 lower, 31, 33, 34 lower, 43, 60, 66, 69, 80, 83, 84–85, 86 lower, 118, 121. Anderson, Rome, p. 42, 76, 79, 91 (2 ×), 92, 93, 119. Arts Graphiques de la Cité, Paris, p. 113, 115 upper. J. Blauel, Munich, p. 99, 175, 205, 213, 214, 216, 222, 245. E. Böhm, Mainz, p. 55, 187, 225 upper, 240 lower, 241. Brogi, Florence, p. 88 lower. Photo Bulloz, Paris, p. 61, 63, 98, 141, 146, 152, 154, 155 lower, 156, 157, 159, 164, 169, 186. Foto J. E. Carrebye, Copenhagen, p. 200. M. Chuzeville, Paris, p. 71 lower, 78. Courtauld Institute of Art, Witt Library, London, p. 7. A. Dingjan, The Hague, p. 182. A. Fréquin, The Hague, p. 170–71, 183, 191 (2 ×), 192, 193, 194, 195, 198. R. Gasparini, Genoa, p. 106. A. Held, Écublens, p. 25, 77, 134. H. Hinz, Basel, p. 209, 218 lower. A. F. Kersting, London, p. 250, 251, 252, 253. Landshut Travel Bureau, p. 230 upper. J. A. Lavaud, Paris, p. 131, 132, 133, 138, 139, 140, 142, 143 (2 ×), 144, 145, 147, 149, 151, 161. A. Luisa, Brescia, p. 48, 49, 51 upper, 52, 57, 58, 62, 115, 120. Bildarchiv Foto Marburg, Marburg, p. 34 upper, 219, 225 lower, 226, 227 upper. E. Meyer, Vienna, p. 72, 87, 114, 123, 158, 180, 185, 223, 236, 237, 238, 239. Nuremberg Travel Bureau, p. 211. M. Pedone, Milan, p. 29 upper, 95. Photo Studios Ltd., London, p. 249. Rapho-Guillumette Pictures, New York, p. 150. J. Remmer, Munich, p. 15, 16, 17, 18–19, 20, 22, 23, 27 (2 ×), 28, 35, 36, 37, 38, 41, 44, 45, 46, 48, 53, 54, 56, 59, 67, 70, 73, 81, 86 upper, 88 upper, 89, 90, 94, 100, 105 (2 ×), 109, 111, 116, 117, 122, 124, 125 (2 ×), 126, 127, 128, 153, 162, 166–67, 172 (2 ×), 173, 179, 196, 206, 207, 212, 215, 218 upper, 220, 231, 233, 234 (2 ×), 235, 243, 246, 247. Rizzoli Archives, Milan, p. 68. W. Rösch, Münster, p. 224, 228–29. Foto Scala, Florence, p. 65, 71 upper, 74, 75, 82, 96, 97, 108. M. Seidel, Mittenwald, p. 203, 217, 240 upper, 242, 244, 247. J. Skeel, Ashford, p. 24, 32, 39, 50, 51 lower, 102, 168. W. Steinkopf, Berlin, p. 40, 110. B. van Gils, Breda, p. 197. R. E. Wolf Archives, Florence, p. 165, 182, 188. The authors and publisher would like to thank all those who have helped to make possible the production of this book, particularly the directors of the various museums and galleries and the photographers.